HOW WASHINGTON REALLY WORKS

FOURTH EDITION

Charles Peters

BASIC
BOOKS

A Member of the Perseus Books Group

Library of Congress Cataloging-in-Publication Data
Peters, Charles, 1926–
    How Washington really works / Charles Peters. —4th ed.
      p. cm.
    Includes index.
    ISBN 0-201-62470-2
    1. United States—Politics and government. 2. Power (Social
sciences) I. Title
JK271.P45   1992
320.973—dc20   92-44602
                                                         CIP

Basic Books is a Member of the Perseus Books Group.

Find us on the World Wide Web at
http://www.basicbooks.com

Cover design by Richard Rossiter
Text design by Debby Jay
Set in 10-point Century Schoolbook by DEKR Corporation, Woburn, MA

Dedicated to the Memory of
Richard Rovere

CONTENTS

INTRODUCTION

Washington, D.C.
January 1, 1993

A few days after Bill Clinton's victory in November, I happened to be on a television talk show with one of the bright young members of his transition staff. His excitement and dedication were transparent and touching. But I was troubled by his confidence, bordering on arrogance, that he and his colleagues were too smart to be taken in by Washington. I remembered that I had felt the same way when I came to work under John Kennedy in 1961, and I realized that one reason I had written this book was to warn other similarly innocent and overconfident newcomers of the things I hadn't known and later learned to wish I had known when I started out in this city.

There are some other members of the Clinton team in whom excessive innocence is clearly not the problem. And they explain two other reasons for writing this book. One is that even seasoned veterans of the Washington scene usually know only the trade secrets of life in the branch in which they serve. Mutual ignorance of one another's world is often embarrassingly obvious when an executive branch witness testifies before Congress. So this book is intended to help the congressman understand the questions he should ask the executive branch, to give the witness an understanding of the pressures on the congressman, and to make each side aware of the games the other is playing.

The final purpose of *How Washington Really Works* is to help the permanent outsider, the Mr. or Ms. Smith who never comes to Washington, understand that most of what our government appears to do is make-believe carried on for the benefit of those in office. The present system is designed to protect those within it not to serve those outside. I hope this book will make the Mr. and Ms. Smiths want to change it. Even if Bill Clinton has the best intentions in the world, he is going to need the strong support of the people to bring about genuine change.

I want to emphasize my belief, because I know this book will sound cynical to many, that the system can be changed. For anybody of my generation, it's necessary only to think back to the early months of our involvement in World War II to realize how dramatically government's performance can improve. Our triumph at Midway in 1942, one of the greatest naval victories in the history of the world, came just six months after the disaster at Pearl Harbor had demonstrated how abysmally inefficient and oblivious to reality government at its worst can be.

Unfortunately, in recent years our system has too often functioned as it did at Pearl Harbor. That is why I have written this book. I want to see more Midways—in the wars against hunger, disease, ignorance, injustice, and war itself, as well as in the military battles we may be unable to avoid. And I know the Midways will happen only if we learn the lessons of the Pearl Harbors.

ACKNOWLEDGMENTS

Regular readers of *The Washington Monthly* will recognize on almost every page my debt to its writers and editors.

I owe special gratitude to my wife, Beth, for her wise counsel, which has been a continuing blessing throughout our life together, and to the late Carol Trueblood, my assistant for 27 years, who was helping me revise this book when she died August 3, 1991.

I also wish to thank Chad Taylor for his assistance in checking facts and for the original research he performed.

FOREWORD

For a great many Americans, Washington no longer seems to work. Like Moslems bowing to Mecca, we keep turning to the capital with hopeful eyes, looking, if not for a miracle, at least for some improvement in our lot in life. When that hope is dashed, we wonder: All that expense, all that calculation, all that exertion of the will—what has it come to? Some disillusioned citizens check all the way out of the great game of politics, having concluded at last that the Washington community is occupied by an essentially foreign power, speaking an alien tongue, addicted to orgies of self-congratulation they have no share in. Politics transforms itself into "us" and "them." "Us" is the American citizens, sprawled in bewilderment across a continent. "Them" is Washington, perpetual generator of useless intrusion and insatiable demand.

The pages you are about to read recount tales of that fabulous city, christened for *the* Founding Father, who, when a quarreling Congress could not decide where to put it, set his finger to the map and located our ruling city. Then Washington existed as a village of ambition: in fact a miserable little swamp, in myth a potential Paris. Foreign diplomats had to be paid extra to serve there. Victors of elections prudently left their families at home. No practical thinker expected it to last past more than one or two of

Jefferson's nineteen-year generations. But then, like Moses rescued from the bulrushes, Washington survived, flourished, established itself, drawing to it national energies beyond the excitement of New York, the rationality of Philadelphia, the dour disdain of Puritan Boston. For better or worse, Washington, District of Columbia, rose from the ashes of the Revolution as our guiding Phoenix, a tattered bird of passage leading into the future, quintessential representative of the vulgar pioneer spirit.

What then went wrong? There are those who attribute our modern malady to the decline of persons, the two-legged human beings who followed in George Washington's footsteps. His city was progressively invaded by lesser lights. Pointy-headed bureaucrats and Claghorn congressmen, not to mention presidents of the Harding mentality, took over and sullied the springs of political virtue. Smarter tyrants followed, and the reaction thereto. The problem of government became the problem of leadership: the search for better men and women to clean up the capital and get the nation moving again.

Just about the time the current new generation of politically conscious Americans appeared in the nurseries, John F. Kennedy appeared in the presidency, a prophet of a higher standard of excellence than had theretofore prevailed. Among those he lured to the nation's capital was one Charles Peters of West Virginia, assigned with consent to find out and tell what the Peace Corps was or was not achieving. What Peters found out was mixed; what he learned to tell was plain. The proof of the pudding in American politics had to do, not with intentions, but with results, real changes in the lives of real people. Peters came to Washington by the great circle route—beginning out there where the programs were meant to make a difference, winding up at the center of action where the programs were made. The gap between results and intentions strained his soul, stimulating wonderment.

Peters, like his familial namesake, was a hoper. Perhaps

the hope really did reside in the Kennedy thrust: recruiting to government service the best and the brightest of a new generation. Perhaps, in alternative, the essential problem was structural: cutting through the red tape of organizational complexity with the knife of decisive, rational reorganization. But the more Charles Peters experienced of Washington, and the more he contemplated the gap between intention and result, the more it dawned on him that he was dealing with something more fundamental than the circulation of elites or the shuffling of structures. Something more powerful. Something visceral. Something at the heart of the enterprise.

Washington had become a culture. Peters perceived that this Capital of Political Culture owed its continued existence to a set of inherited modes of belief and expectation that gripped the city's practitioners at least as powerfully as did the organization charts. Washington really worked by a set of mores—values thought natural—increasingly divergent from the country's common sense. *That* was the crisis of the twentieth century's waning years: a crisis of vision. Inside the capital city, isolated from the criteria of performance the rest of us took for granted, a peculiar tribal ethic had developed, subject to anthropological analysis, a myopic morality of the salon. The rest of "us" had better understand how that ethic works, because it is where the power is.

For all his skepticism, Charles Peters remains an inveterate hoper. His vision sights forward, toward a humane, decent, practical society where doing the right thing is not the exception but the rule.

We think he would travel with Emerson: "When it gets dark enough you can see the stars." With him, we hope so.

JAMES DAVID BARBER
*James B. Duke Professor of Political
Science at Duke University*

HOW
WASHINGTON
REALLY
WORKS

1.

THE PRESS

The first key to understanding Washington is "make-believe." Washington is like the Winter Palace under Nicholas and Alexandra, where earnest discussions of the lot of the poor went on continually but the discussions were seldom accompanied by effective action. In Washington bureaucrats confer, the president proclaims, and Congress legislates, but the effect on reality is usually negligible if evident at all. The nation's problems don't disappear, and all the activity that is supposedly dedicated to their solution turns out to be make-believe.

All too often the press, instead of exposing this make-believe, is part of the show. It dutifully covers the apparent action—the announcement of programs, the enactment of legislation—rather than finding out how the programs are executed and the legislation is implemented or what the government is *not* doing about crucial problems.

Suppose, for example, a mine safety bill is being considered by Congress. There is little possibility that the press, even C-Span, will cover the committee hearings. What will probably happen is there will be little or no coverage until the bill's passage is near, when there might be a story briefly summarizing the positions of the bill's advocates and opponents and appraising the likelihood of passage. When the bill is passed, a reporter may appear on the evening news, standing on the Capitol steps and solemnly intoning, "Today Congress passed the Mine Safety Act of 1993." A week or so thereafter we may see another reporter standing on the White House lawn saying, "Today the president signed the Mine Safety Act of 1993." But all that denotes is the appearance of action. Nothing has yet happened in the mines. And it is almost certain that no reporter will go down into the mines to find out. Thus the reality of what happened, whether the bill made the mines more safe or less, will not be investigated or reported—until there is a major mine disaster somewhere in Appalachia.

Readers who doubt this scenario might consider what happened when the savings and loans were deregulated during the eighties. Can they recall any of the national press going out to visit individual S&Ls to find out what was going on? They might also consider this revealing recollection of a former assistant secretary of what is now Health and Human Services, Eileen Shannahan: "Of the many times I tried to interest distinguished reporters from distinguished publications in the effort the department was making to find out whether its billion-dollar programs actually were reaching the intended beneficiaries and doing any good, their eyes glazed over."

There is no better example of journalism as part of the show than the press conference. The appearance is adversarial—tough reporters asking tough questions. The reality is far different. "We tried to identify people to ask softball questions," writes Ronald Reagan's press aide, Larry Speakes, in his book "Speaking Out." And Reagan, instead of giving spontaneous answers to those questions, was rehearsed by his staff so that he would reply in the way least likely to give political offense.

George Bush, who felt more comfortable and confident dealing with foreign rather than domestic policy, was successful at controlling the topics raised at his press conferences. According to a study conducted by *The Washington Monthly*'s James Bennet, fully two-thirds of the questions asked at presidential press conferences between January 1989 and September 1991 were about foreign affairs. Amazingly, this tally excluded conferences devoted to the Gulf War where questions about foreign policy would have been expected to dominate. During the same period, Bush answered only four questions about AIDS and only two questions about the dozens of bank failures—the kind of questions he didn't like.

"In press conferences, out of 30 questions we might fail to anticipate one," says Speakes. And this is true not only of the White House but of the press conferences held by other top government officials as well. Lt. General Thomas Kelly, the Pentagon's chief briefer during the 1991 Gulf War, recalls that one of his press conferences turned out to be so close to the rehearsal that he jokingly asked an assistant if he'd given the practice questions to the reporters.

"What was stunning was not what tripped me up," Kelly explains, "but how over prepared I was for the usual range of questions."

Hodding Carter, who served as the State Department's spokesman throughout the Carter years, including the hostage crisis, says "I can't remember a dozen times that I was caught unprepared."

One of the reasons for the persistence of make-believe is the press's traditional "beat" system. Reporters are assigned regularly to the White House, to Congress, to the Pentagon, and to the State Department. They cover official pronouncements, but only rarely do they find out whether the savings and loans are being regulated properly or the poor are being fed and housed. Tom Wicker of the *New York Times* explains:

"The problem . . . is that the American press tends to be an institutionalized press. It covers institutions and official spokesmen and official visible functions. When I was a bureau chief in Washington, I had roughly 30 reporters to deploy around town, and I know how hard it is to get away from the 'beat' system. When they are sent out to cover institutions and spokesmen [which is what the beat system does], they inevitably miss a lot of other things that are happening."

The government likes the beat system as much as the reporters do. Every high official has a press secretary or public information officer, who in turn often has his own platoon—and sometimes army—of assistants. Here are the numbers of government employees who were involved in public relations work at some of the more important government offices as of September 30, 1989:

Agriculture	513	EPA	91
Health and Human		Energy	89
Services	266	Transportation	74
Treasury	212	Justice	60
Interior	155	Commerce	59
Tennessee Valley		State	59
Authority	135	Veterans' Affairs	56
NASA	116	Labor	54

There are 750 press secretaries on Capitol Hill. But even that number is dwarfed by the army of press handlers at the Pentagon, which currently has 1,590 members.

All these people make it easy for a reporter to get the news they want him to get. They issue press releases almost every day to make sure reporters are aware of whatever their bosses have said or done that can be made to look good. And they coddle reporters in a warm cocoon of perquisites. Here, as described in a *Washington Monthly* article, is a typical day for journalists who cover Congress:

"First stop, the Senate press gallery. It's more spacious than the gallery on the House side of the Capitol. There is time to settle into one of the big, old leather chairs to read a copy or two of the 10 daily newspapers supplied us by the

Congress. Browsing completed, it's back out past the uniformed guard at the gallery door.

"On your way to some morning coffee, you take the "Press/ Staff Only" elevator down to one of the Senate cafeterias. Similar to the "Senators Only" elevator, it runs about a floor faster than the public elevators. There is a special section reserved for the press in the cafeteria. Around the corner, the public waits in a long line for a chance to eat breakfast in a Senate restaurant. Here, it's time to engage in colloquy with your colleagues, to discuss the issues of the day and what The Leadership is doing. We could linger, but there is a hearing to cover for the newspaper back home.

"Arriving at the hearing room, you are greeted by another uniformed fellow, who waves you through once you produce your congressional gallery pass. You squeeze by several dozen other people who are standing in line to. enter. . . . Once inside, a Senate gallery staff member escorts you to the seat you requested yesterday. Ahead of all others who might be affected by the legislation being considered at the hearing, you are provided copies of testimony by the same gallery staff member. After the hearing you return to the gallery to bat out a quick story. The typewriter and paper are provided by Congress.

"Off to the House side, where debate has started on the floor on some question or other of great national importance. During debate you may be summoned to the gallery office for telephone calls, which are dutifully logged for you by the gallery staff. The long bank of telephone booths has been provided for in the congressional budget. . . .

"It could be an anniversary, a birthday, or maybe it's Christmas. You've forgotten someone. It's all right. One of the nicest things about serving the people's right to know is the Senate stationery store, where members, staff, *and* reporters can shop at prices below retail."

"As evening falls on Washington, you return to your car, which is parked in spaces bestowed by the House Administration Committee and the Senate Rules Committee." Today garage parking on Capitol Hill costs $1620 a year when it is available. But permit-holding reporters park free in the press spaces provided by the Congress.

Reporters assigned to the Defense Department get a lot more than free parking and leather chairs: The Pentagon will fly them anywhere, whether across the country or around the world, to cover the stories it wants them to print. The White House sometimes even arranges for reporters' families to go along on presidential trips—at one-third to one-half the cost of ordinary fares—to places like Santa Barbara and Kennebunkport.

During the Gulf War reporters were housed in luxury hotels like the five-star Dharan International at which the pool side area where the TV cameras were set up was called "Little Hollywood" and those blue domes you saw in the background were not mosques but cabanas.

The reporters' part of the bargain is to participate in the make-believe that real news is being made in these places rather than just routine statements between rounds of golf.

Because officials are so anxious to get good press, there is often tremendous pressure on the government press agent. Shortly after Robert McKinney became chairman of the Federal Home Loan Bank Board, in the early days of the Carter administration, his public relations officer, Mike Scanlon, arranged a press briefing that put McKinney on the front page of both the *Washington Post* and the *New York Times*. It wasn't long before McKinney came to expect that kind of coverage all the time. When he made a speech in San Francisco that received local publicity but none back East, he fired Scanlon.

Don McClure recalls the time he was serving as public relations officer for the Peace Corps under Sargent Shriver: "One week three magazines—*Newsweek, Look,* and the *Saturday Evening Post*—hit the stands with Peace Corps stories. Shriver wanted to know why we weren't in *Time*."

With government press agents operating under this kind of pressure, Washington reporters find stories easy to get.

The problem is that they're often too easy to get. People who have reached the top levels of government have usually attained their positions at least partly through their skill in handling journalists. They know how to make themselves look good, and they also know how to divert attention from the less flattering stories. Reporters who become dependent on these officials, as most do, simply don't get the truth about what's wrong. The most spectacular example of this failure is the case of the White House press corps during the unfolding of the Watergate and Iran-contra scandals. Not one of the scores of journalists assigned to full-time coverage of the White House played any part in breaking these stories. They had been spoon-fed for so long that they had lost the habit of independent inquiry.

The men who got the Watergate story, Bob Woodward and Carl Bernstein of the *Washington Post,* did not get it by asking questions of the White House press office. One of their sources, Deep Throat, is widely suspected to have been David Gergen, a low-ranking functionary in the Nixon White House who later handled publicity for the Reagan administration. The other Deep Throat suspects—Fred Fielding, the deputy counsel, and Alexander Haig, the National Security Council deputy at the time Watergate began—did not belong at the top of the White House pecking order with such stars of the era as H. R. Haldeman, John Erlichman, Charles Colson and Henry Kissinger. The sources whose identities Woodward and Bernstein later revealed were not high-ranking officials either; they were personal secretaries and middle-level executives, like Hugh Sloan, the assistant treasurer of the Committee to Re-elect the President. When Bill Moyers was press secretary to Lyndon Johnson, he said the kind of leaker Johnson feared most was not the cabinet member, who could usually be trusted to guard his comments even after infuriatingly disappointing sessions with the president. Rather, Moyers said, the cabinet member's special assistant, who heard every-

thing about those sessions once the cabinet member returned to his office, was much more likely to be the source
of a leak.

Similarly, in the case of the Challenger disaster, the people who could have blown the whistle if reporters had asked
were middle-level officials, like Richard Cook at NASA and
Allan McDonald of Thiokol, who saw the danger but were
ignored by both their bosses and the press. The savings and
loan scandal could have been cracked early on if reporters
had interviewed federal examiners such as Charles Black,
who was going over the books of the shaky thrifts. And
Reagan's knowledge of Iran-contra might have been exposed
if they had just queried a navy enlisted man named James
R. Radzimski, whom Seymour Hersh finally got around to
talking to in 1990.

Such lower-level subordinates are more prone to talk because they are several layers removed from personal loyalty
to the president and because they are less skilled than their
bosses in fending off the questions of the press. There is
another factor that sometimes encourages them to be honest: loyalty to something they see as being more important
than the president. This could be the welfare of the country,
or it could simply be the welfare of their agency. The reporter who, next to Woodward and Bernstein, did the best
job on Watergate, Sandy Smith of *Time,* got most of his
material from middle-level bureaucrats at the FBI who re-
sented Patrick Gray's attempt to make what they regarded
as political use of the bureau. And don't forget James
McCord's famous letter to Judge Sirica that broke the Watergate dam. It was motivated by McCord's anger at what
Nixon had tried to do to the CIA, where McCord had been
a middle-level bureaucrat.

It can be argued that Woodward and Bernstein got the
Watergate story precisely because they were not White
House correspondents but local reporters for the *Washington
Post*'s Metro section. If they had been White House corre-

spondents, they would have asked Nixon's press secretary, Ron Ziegler, and other top White House officials what was going on and received the usual runaround. Because they weren't, they had to dig down to the lower-level people who knew the story and were willing to talk.

The people who work on the Metro section of the *Post* have since often tried to follow Woodward and Bernstein's example and make their reputations by uncovering a scandal. But once a Metro reporter has "made it," he gets assigned to a prestigious national affairs beat. Unfortunately, the reporter then tends to become a statesman covering other statesmen. This is exactly what happened to Woodward and Bernstein themselves. For the inside information in their second book, *The Final Days,* they relied heavily on Alexander Haig and Fred Buzhardt, who were high-level officials during the last year of the Nixon administration. Buzhardt had replaced John Dean as White House Counsel and Haig, who had left his deputy's post at the NSC to return to the Army, had been called back by Nixon to serve as White House Chief of Staff when H. R. Haldeman resigned. Not surprisingly, the book makes both Haig and Buzhardt appear to be fine fellows if not outright heroes. In fact, both were far from being innocent bystanders in the conspiracy to obstruct justice that was the main activity of the White House during Nixon's last two years as president.

Unfortunately, with the notable exception of *The Brethren,* which he co-authored with Scott Armstrong, Woodward was to continue to rely on big-shot sources for his later books, including *Veil* (source, CIA Director William Casey) and *The Commanders* (sources, Secretary of Defense Dick Cheney and Chairman of the Joint Chiefs Colin Powell). When Woodward and David Broder published their 1992 book about Dan Quayle, the *Washington Post* journalism critic observed that "The authors devoted an extraordinary amount of space to the comments Quayle made during 20 interviews."

Syndicated columnists are particularly susceptible to being conned by their important sources. Because they have to turn out several columns a week, they don't have time to piece together stories from dozens of interviews. Talking to a few top officials who supposedly know the whole story is therefore irresistibly appealing. (When Tom Braden was embarking on his career as a Washington columnist, one of the reigning journalistic eminences of the era, Stewart Alsop, advised him to be sure to talk to three important people each day.) In addition, readers are impressed by exclusive interviews with world leaders, all of which inflates the columnist's own sense of self-importance. Soon it is beneath him even to consider doing any legwork or talking to those more lowly who might tell him something really interesting.

The heights to which this self-importance can rise were illustrated during the Reagan administration, when George Will was invited to a Christmas party hosted by then vice president George Bush. When Will's secretary called to inquire if "the press will be present," the answer was yes, and the secretary responded, "Mr. Will does not attend events where press are invited."

Will is also an excellent example of how closeness to a source can affect a journalist. In 1980, speaking on television after a Reagan-Carter debate, Will praised Reagan's performance. He did not disclose that he had privately helped Reagan prepare for the debate. And in early 1987, in the middle of the Iran-contra scandal, I was having lunch at Galileo's, a Washington restaurant, and noticed Will and Nancy Reagan locked in earnest conversation at a nearby table. The next night I happened to be watching the ABC Evening News as Peter Jennings turned to Will and asked whether he had discussed Iran-contra with the Reagans. Will answered, "No, I haven't seen them lately."

The trap, as we saw with Woodward and Bernstein's treatment of Haig and Buzhardt, is that the columnist becomes obligated to give his source favorable treatment. He becomes the prisoner of his source. The more access he is given, the harder it is to criticize. The late Drew Pearson, author of "The Washington Merry-Go-Round," said, "We will give immunity to a very good source as long as the information he offers us is better than what we have on him." Michael Deaver is a prime example of how this works. While he was in the Reagan White House and regularly leaking stories to his favorite reporters, Lou Cannon of the *Washington Post* and Laurence Barrett of *Time*, scarcely a bad word was said about him in either publication. But once he resigned and went into public relations, he became fair game and many unfavorable stories about him appeared in both. Similarly, as Jonathan Alter revealed in 1987, Oliver North had been a favorite and protected source of such publications as *Newsweek, Time*, and the *New York Times* until the Iran-contra scandal became so big that he could no longer be protected.

In this connection it is interesting to note that Michael Deaver's rivals for the title of biggest leaker during the Reagan administration's first term, James Baker and Richard Darman, continued to receive favorable treatment from the press, especially those reporters who regularly covered them and depended on them as sources. Unlike Deaver, they remained in power and maintained their value as sources well into Reagan's second term, then quickly returned to the government as members of the Bush administration in 1989.

James Baker's protected status as a favorite source was illustrated by the story of the $2.9 million worth of stock he held in the Chemical National Bank, which he did not disclose while, as secretary of the treasury in Reagan's second term, he was making decisions favoring major banks like Chemical. If a Bert Lance or an Ed Meese had been guilty of the same thing, editorials demanding his head would have appeared, followed by a congressional investigation and the appointment of a special prosecutor. But when word of Baker's holdings finally got out in early 1989 there was hardly a murmur from the reporters, who were so dependent on him that they could not face losing the leaks he provided.

Reporters have good reason to fear the anger of good sources. When Larry Speakes was upset by an item in a *Washington Times* gossip column alleging that Nancy Reagan wanted to get rid of him, he ostracized Jeremiah O'Leary, the paper's White House correspondent, until the editor of the *Times* informed him that the columnist's contract was not being renewed. What most troubles me about this episode is that I happen to know the White House source who gave the gossip item to the *Times* well enough to know it must have been true. Thus O'Leary was punished for printing the truth. Similarly, *Newsweek* was cut off by George Bush after it ran its "Wimp Factor" cover during the 1988 primaries. Some of its reporters felt that *Newsweek* subsequently took excessive care not to offend Bush after he won the election.

Bush was probably more upset by leaks than any president in recent history. A source identified by the *Washington Post* as "a Republican familiar with the workings of the Reagan and Bush administrations" said:

"A lot of the way the White House operates is based on the leaks thing. I think you know how obsessed George Bush is about leaks. What you don't know is the fullness of the obsession. It's right up there as one of his core values. You know, service, religion, leaks. You don't understand how much time they spend making sure Bush's secrets stay secret and then doing a who-shot-John when they don't."

Baker and Darman escaped punishment not only because their leaks seldom injured Bush but also because Bush thought he needed their services. But less exalted leakers had to beware. One reason Craig Fuller did not remain George Bush's chief of staff after the 1988 campaign was that he was suspected of leaking like a sieve to David Hoffman of the *Washington Post,* a reporter whom George Bush happened to dislike especially.

By 1985, a historic development in the Washington press corps was clear enough for Charlotte Hays and Jonathan Rowe to describe in an article in *The Washington Monthly* called "Reporters: The New Washington Elite" and for James Fallows to expand on the same theme eleven months later in "The New Celebrities of Washington," in the *New York Review of Books*. Simply put, reporters began to worry more about getting on talk shows than reporting, and more about coming up with catchy comments than finding out what was really going on.

Woodward and Bernstein had already given journalism glamour and status with the Watergate story. Then television conferred stardom on the reporters on "60 Minutes" as well as the panelists on various discussion shows. There was something good about the recognition of the hard-digging that Woodward and Bernstein and the "60 Minutes" people had done. But when the panel show pontificators became celebrities, commanding huge fees on the lecture circuit, something very bad happened to journalism. As John Herbers, an editor of *Governing* magazine and for many years a Washington correspondent for the *New York Times* put it, "The prevailing orientation of Washington journalists began to change from populist, working middle class to moneyed elite in the early seventies."

The result of this change, says Hodding Carter, a columnist for the *Wall Street Journal,* is that:

"The top journalists move in packs with the affluent and powerful in Washington. They swarm with them in the summer to every agreeable spot on the eastern seaboard [the favorite spots seem to be the Hamptons and Martha's Vineyard]. When any three or four of them sit down together on a television talk show, it is not difficult to remember that the least well paid of these pontificators make at least six times more each year than the average American family. The truth is that there is not a hell of a lot of tolerance or empathy among the leading figures of national journalism for outsiders, losers, nonconformists, or seriously provocative political figures or causes."

Those television talk shows have been a significant factor in the increasing prosperity of American journalists. Appearances on the shows translate into popularity on the lecture circuit, where by the late eighties the leading star, George Will, was making $15,000 for each speech. Pat Buchanan's income for 1991 exceeded $800,000.

Morton Kondracke wrote a story in which he criticized Senator Lloyd Bentsen for wanting to charge lobbyists $10,000 to have breakfast with him. But Kondracke sees nothing wrong with asking lobbyists to pay $5,000 to hear Morton Kondracke speak. He refuses to reveal his own earnings from such speeches and has condemned financial disclosure for journalists as "an exercise in voyeurism and an invasion of privacy."

Not only are their political views influenced by their rising prosperity, but according to Joe Cosby, a Washington agent who handles bookings for speakers, the tendency to move to the right has been reinforced by the fact that the lecture invitations require not only that the speaker "be on television" but that he also "be conservative."

One reason the press is unlikely to express unconventional wisdom is that today's press lords tend to be conventional people who see themselves as stewards rather than as messiahs. What the Sulzbergers and the Grahams fear most is embarrassing error, so they select people for their staffs who are not likely to embarrass them.

The thinking done by today's journalists is thus unlikely to err on the side of originality. There is, in fact, a considerable amount of intellectual insecurity in the press room. Reporters are often reluctant to examine substantive issues. If they do they instinctively embrace the conventional wisdom. But they really prefer reporting the horse-race aspects of politics—who's ahead in the latest poll—to dealing with candidates' positions. They prefer writing about gaffes and scandals to trying to figure out if a candidate is right in what he proposes to do about national defense or social security. If forced to deal with issues, they will quote experts. The political scientist Norman Ornstein was crowned King of Quotes by *The Washington Monthly* in 1986 because reporters had come to rely on him so much to tell them what to think.

The discipline that journalists have been most diffident about is economics. This, in addition to their distaste for leaving Washington to pursue stories at the grass roots, explains their failure to get the savings and loan story in time to prevent disaster. They simply felt they didn't have the expertise to pursue the story. The ignorance of economics is so great that even one of the more intelligent TV reporters, Ted Koppel, devoted only six out of 1,850 of his shows to the deficit during the eighties when it was growing by $1.6 trillion.

Another common failure of reporting are articles about alleged abuses in which the significance of the abuse isn't made clear. Conflicts of interest are reported as evil per se, when they are only potentially evil. (When a reporter reveals that a senator owns stock in a company that does business with the government, for instance, he too often stops there, with merely finding the conflict of interest, instead of proceeding to determine whether the conflict has ever actually influenced the senator's official behavior—which is the real story.)

Worst of all for Washington, the investigative reporter looks for scandalous illegality when he should be looking into why the government doesn't work. What's wrong with government today seldom has much to do with illegality. Occasionally it does, such as when a congressman is on the take, ABSCAM, or when officials in the General Services Administration are taking bribes from government suppliers. But most of the time the explanation of what is wrong lies in the cultures of the bureaucracy, Congress, the White House, and the judiciary—that is, in the customs and rituals and pressures that govern conduct in these institutions. The average reporter is remarkably ignorant of these cultures.

Reporters who understand the culture of the bureaucracy would have known, for example, that one or more tragedies like My Lai were likely to occur in Vietnam as soon as the Pentagon began publishing body counts of enemy casualties to prove America was winning the war. Reporters would have realized that the pressure for more casualties would lead commanders to find those casualties wherever they could. If reporters had understood that mentality, they would not have waited for the story to be revealed by a Vietnam veteran a year after the fact. They might even have prevented it by asking questions and writing stories about the dangerous possibility that the numbers game would lead to shooting women, children, water buffalo—anything that could be counted in the casualty totals.

Another example: In May 1978 the *Washington Post* ran a front-page scandal story telling how one government agency had spent money recklessly at the end of the fiscal year in order to use up all of its appropriation and avoid risking a budget cut because it hadn't spent all its funds. Neither the author of the article nor the editor knew that the end-of-year spending spree has been a government-wide practice for years. Here journalists at one of the nation's leading newspapers—one that has long had primary responsibility for covering Washington—were unaware of an important facet of the culture of the bureaucracy.

The problem continues into the 1990s. Consider how long it took the Pentagon press corps to wake up to the big way they were being conned by the reported 80 percent success rate of air missions in the Gulf. They even failed to understand when Colin Powell gave away the key to the hustle on the first day by explaining that the rate was based on "arriving at the target and delivering the ordnance." If the reporters had had the experience in government to give them a first-hand feel for the con, they would have noticed that there was no mention of the ordnance hitting the target.

The importance of bureaucratic experience to the reporter was never better illustrated than by an article Donald Graham, now the publisher of the *Washington Post,* wrote in 1990 about the Washington police department that drew on Graham's own experience as a cop twenty years earlier:

"Amazingly, the department still has a promotion system in which effectiveness at a patrolman's job has nothing to do with promotion. Who makes sergeant is based partly on an exam and partly on a brief interview with two police officials and a citizen, who are supposed to be unacquainted with the officer they're interviewing. . . ."

Reading Graham's article led me to write in *The Washington Monthly*:

"Donald Graham must know that because of his experience, he understands a lot about police work that his reporters don't. Why not expand that lesson and require that new *Post* reporters be hired at least partly on the basis of having real experience in government and the other areas they cover? I have found that nothing has meant more to me as a journalist covering government than my experience in the federal bureaucracy and before that as a state legislator, lawyer, and soldier. Knowing what it's really like on the inside gives one a sense of where the bodies are buried and what are the right questions to ask."

In addition to looking for the crooks and covering "politics," reporters should be trying to understand the system. This would not only make it possible for them to explain how and why the occasional official crook becomes crooked, but it could also allow an examination of the much more significant problem of how and why good and decent men could produce an inefficient, uncaring, and sometimes evil government.

The real story behind Vietnam, for example, was available to many reporters in Washington. After all, those who had friends at the State Department knew most of them were privately against the war from the day it started until the day it ended. Why didn't these officials say at work what they confided to friends at dinner parties? Because they were afraid of damaging their careers. And why didn't their journalist friends report what was said privately? Because they were in the same survival network and did not want to hurt the officials' careers.

When the *New York Review of Books* sent Mary McCarthy, the noted writer-intellectual, to Vietnam in 1967 to find out why the war was still going on, she said that she hadn't gone earlier because her husband was in the foreign service and she didn't want to endanger his position. She didn't even have to go to Vietnam; she could have gotten the story from her husband—and from herself. Why hadn't he resigned in protest, or why hadn't she reported his failure to do so? Looked at that way, she might have found the war criminals more understandable.

The influence of the press on government officials cannot be overestimated. This influence can be positive. Think how much chicanery dies on the drawing board when someone says, "We'd better not do that—what if the press finds out?" On the other hand, there are ill effects:

• A public official or a candidate for public office seldom does anything important after five o'clock because it won't make the evening news and therefore will not have "happened."

• Presidential candidates campaign in the small, out-of-the-way state of New Hampshire because they know reporters are watching the results of New Hampshire's early primary closely.

• Top staff meetings at the White House and in the various agencies and departments are devoted to getting puff pieces written. The puff pieces are then accepted as reality by those who inspired them.

• The transcripts of meetings of the Nuclear Regulatory

Commission just after the near disaster at Three Mile Island indicate that the only time the commissioners devoted sustained attention to one subject was when they debated— sometimes for hours—the wording of a press release. And this during a period when life-and-death decisions affecting hundreds of thousands of people had to be made.

Washington reporters *could* find out the truth. It doesn't require unusual ability—just the willingness to break free of the conventional beats and go where the real action is. But they are too bound up in the make-believe system of reporting apparent action, in the ease of being stenographers for government press agents, and in the thrill of rubbing shoulders with the mighty and walking through the White House gate past the admiring eyes of waiting tourists.

Never are the journalist's real motives so nakedly exposed as at the annual White House correspondents dinner, at which reporters compete to get top officials to sit at their tables so that their editors and publishers will be impressed with just how well connected their own correspondents are. At the correspondents dinner in 1990, for example, guests at the *New York Times* table included two cabinet members, a White House staff member, budget director Richard Darman, and Jesse Jackson. Reporters will also go to desperate lengths to get invitations to the White House Christmas party. CNN's Candy Crowley, then with Associated Press, once pleaded, "My boss won't let me off on Christmas and New Year's unless you invite him."

When William Kovach was chief of the Washington bureau of the *New York Times* he remarked, "Nothing is more painful than the look on the face of a reporter who has been told that he or she must turn in the White House press pass because someone else needs it more, nor is there any look quite as seraphic as that on the face of one told he or she has just been added to the list of White House press pass holders." White House reporters will cynically tell you (off the record, of course) all about being spoon-fed by the president's press secretary. They don't say it on the record because they don't want their editors to see it and take them off the White House beat. They know that what they're doing doesn't really count, but the folks back home think it does. It sometimes seems that White House reporters live for the stories they can tell their friends—anecdotes about Bush and Gorbachev or Kennedy and his girlfriends. It may be only make-believe, but as the press plane takes off for another presidential trip abroad, who cares?

2.

LOBBIES

"Dear Dick," the letter began. "As I told you on the telephone, our firm has represented ITT . . . since its incorporation over 50 years ago." The letter was addressed to Richard Kleindienst, then deputy attorney general. It was written by Lawrence Walsh, known in the 1990s as the Special Prosecutor in the Iran-Contra cases but prominent years earlier as a former deputy attorney general, a former federal judge, and, when he wrote the letter, a Wall Street lawyer representing ITT. Walsh was asking Kleindienst to do a favor for his client. The favor, which opened the door for ITT to settle an antitrust suit in a way that let the conglomerate keep the assets it wanted most, was granted. When Kleindienst was asked why he went along, he explained: "It was the relationship I had with Judge Walsh, the fact that he was a former deputy attorney general. . . . He wasn't an ordinary attorney as far as I'm concerned."

Kleindienst and Walsh had a special relationship because they were both members of the same "club": present and former high officials of the Justice Department. Kleindienst knew that he too would someday be a former deputy attorney general, and consciously or unconsciously, he was treat-

25

ing Walsh the way *he* wished to be treated on his return to private practice. By taking care of ITT's "little problem," Kleindienst added another link to a great chain of favors, a quid pro quo that both men understood without having to specify a form for Kleindienst's future *quo*.

Kleindienst's favor to ITT became public—and controversial—because it became enmeshed in the larger Watergate scandal. But by Washington standards, even by post-Watergate standards, what Kleindienst did was not scandalous. After all, he received no money from Walsh. His action was the simple, straightforward result of successful lobbying, and hundreds of similar incidents take place in Washington every business day.

The narrow, legal definition of a lobbyist, as prescribed by the federal lobbying act, is one who "solicits, collects, or receives contributions where one of the main purposes is to influence the passage or defeat of congressional legislation and the intended method of accomplishing the purpose is through conversation with members of Congress." This definition, however, has more loopholes than a spiral notebook. It leaves out for example, people who lobby the executive branch; organizations that can show that lobbying is not their main purpose in raising money; individuals or groups who use their own money to influence legislation; and those who don't personally approach members of Congress. In 1991, a Senate subcommittee reported that, of $5.7 million spent on lobbying by six military contractors, only $3,547 had to be reported. And although there are approximately one hundred thousand people working directly or indirectly as lobbyists in Washington, only about seventy-three hundred are registered under federal law.

But there are really millions of lobbyists. When you write your congressman, you are lobbying: broadly speaking, lobbying is any attempt to influence the action of a public official. Private individuals and corporations lobby the executive branch as well as Congress, as do groups representing various causes or even the "public interest." In addition, the branches lobby each other: Congressmen try to influence executive or agency decisions, and the White House lobbies Congress to support its proposals.

The popular conception of a lobbyist is someone who passes money under the table, arranges for clandestine midnight assignations, or holds the threat of blackmail not very high over an official's head. In fact, much of the activity that falls within the broad definition of lobbying is not evil, or even underhanded. When you write a federal official to express an opinion on some public issue, you are trying to make democracy work. You know perfectly well, however, that your letter is not likely to get much attention, so you consider various actions to make sure attention *is* paid. One way could be to give a cash bribe. But old Washington hands have developed more subtle lobbying techniques, which are equally effective and have the added advantage of being legal.

The story of Richard Kleindienst and Judge Walsh illustrates the most effective legal way of influencing a public official: having something in common, being a member of the same "club." The most obvious of these clubs is composed of officials' personal friends. This is why in 1990 Philip Morris began to hire lobbyists from the hometowns of congressmen. The Philip Morris lobbyist in Sioux Falls, South Dakota, for example, happens to be a longtime friend of Senator Thomas Daschle, who as a member of the Senate Finance Committee could vote against taxes on tobacco. The friendship connection also explains why Thomas "Lud" Ashley was the hottest Washington lobbyist of the early nineties. He is a close friend of George Bush. Ashley is also a former congressman, which makes him a member of another important club. At latest count, made by the *National Journal* in 1989, seventy-six former congressmen are working as Washington lobbyists.

The mutual membership can even be in an actual Washington club like Burning Tree (golf) or the Metropolitan (lunch). Burning Tree forbids lobbying on its premises, but the friendships formed there have been central to many lobbyists' success. Charls (yes, that's the way he spells it) Walker, one of the most successful corporate lobbyists of the seventies and eighties, plays a lot of golf at Burning Tree.

At the Metropolitan Club in downtown Washington, members bask in the glow conferred by the combination of money, power, and social position held by the people who are present each day in the dining room. Sometimes merely taking a federal official to lunch there so he can share in the glow a little while is enough to win his sympathetic attention.

Clubs are just part of a larger social bond that exists everywhere but is especially prevalent in Washington, where private life is so much an extension of professional life. This bond is the "survival network," and it is another key to understanding how Washington really works.

Almost everyone in the government, whether he works on Capitol Hill or in the bureaucracy, is concerned primarily with his own survival. He wants to remain in Washington or in what the city symbolizes—some form of public power. So, from the day he arrives in Washington he is busy building networks of people who will ensure his survival in power. The smart lobbyist knows he must build networks not only for himself but for those officials he tries to influence. Each time the lobbyist meets an official whose help he needs, he tries to let him know—in the most subtle ways possible—that he can be an important part of that official's survival network.

Suppose you are elected to Congress and are invited to dinner by a clever lobbyist. You will find that as soon as you walk into his living room and the introductions begin, you are meeting one person after another who can be valuable to your career. If, say, you are interested in protecting a defense base or industry in your district the guest list might include the Secretary of Defense, Dick Cheney, and the Chairman of the House Armed Services Committee, Les Aspin. And since all congressmen like to get to know the press, there will probably be a reporter from the *Washington Post* or the *New York Times*. Because you are also likely to be valuable to your new acquaintances, friendships develop. And in the long run the friendships formed in these social situations can be a powerful force in decision making. Indeed, there are times when the lobbyist will act more out of loyalty to his network than to his client. He knows that the folks at Mobil or Exxon may forget him one day, but his network won't. This is one of those complex truths about Washington that conventional analysts from either the left or the right rarely see. And it is a truth that helps explain why lobbyists go into lobbying. They are surviving.

Most of the best lobbyists are former high government officials—ex-congressmen, ex-White House staff members, ex-cabinet officers, and ex-assistant secretaries. They usually entered public service with no thought of later turning it to their own advantage, and most at first probably planned to return home after their government service ended. But when actually faced with the prospect of going back, they discover that they now think of Washington as home. Their friends are there, their children are in local schools, they own houses in the area. Above all, they are hooked on the sense of excitement, of being at the center of events, that living in the capital confers on its residents. They want to stay in that world, but they have only one really marketable skill that can allow them to remain— their knowledge of government. So they become lobbyists. Their friends who are still in government realize that the same thing may eventually happen to them, and they take care to be considerate when the lobbyists come calling.

Although it is a by-product of the survival instinct, this empathy is genuine. It tightens and reinforces the bonds of everyone's network so that, as Nicholas Lemann observed in *The Washington Monthly,* "although Washington is supposed to be a city where power is carefully balanced between groups with contradictory interests, in fact it's a place with a strong sense of shared enterprise, a place where every person you deal with is someone who is either helping you survive now or might conceivably later on."

The reason that membership in a club is such an effective lobbying tool is that very often the key to effective lobbying is simply *access*. If you are a former congressman, belonging to the club of present and former members gives you an actual physical advantage in the access race: The floor of the House and Senate and legislators' private dining rooms are open to former members and no other lobbyists.

Why is access so vital? If the other side can't get similar access, a lobbyist's views may be all an official ever hears. Especially on smaller issues, where a decision either way won't rock the ship of state, whichever side gets to a congressman usually wins. This can also be true on larger and more controversial issues in nonelection years, when officials care less about public opinion. Even when the congressman hears other views, the voice of a friend is likely to stand out in the cacophony of opinions.

More insidious, the psychology of access plays on the fact that most government officials are basically decent people who want to be nice and to be liked. Faced with a living, breathing fellow human being who wants something very much, and with perhaps only an abstract argument on the other side, the natural reaction is to be obliging. That's why, if you are a lobbyist, just getting through to a high official and presenting your case, using facts, figures, and persuasion—no favors involved—gives you a good chance of success. In fact, this is the way most lobbying victories are won.

Between club and cash there is a wide variety of techniques for gaining access to and influence with the public official whose decisions may affect the lobbyist's company, administration, constituents, or cause. There's the innocent favor, for instance—helping the official's son get a summer job, helping his daughter get into Smith, or introducing him to the social, sports, literary, or entertainment celebrities he happens to admire. Nothing of tangible value is exchanged, yet gratitude is earned.

A story about the late Andy Biemiller, a congressman who became an extremely effective congressional lobbyist for the AFL-CIO, is an excellent example of how effective the innocent favor can be. Biemiller knew that a certain congressman was faced with a serious operation. He knew that George Meany, then head of the AFL-CIO, had needed the same operation and found an outstanding doctor who successfully performed the difficult surgery. Biemiller referred the congressman to this doctor, who again worked his magic. Meany followed up with a personal call. The result: The congressman, who had voted against labor before he became ill, voted with labor on an important measure that came up just after he left the hospital.

The insidiousness of the innocent favor is that, like access, it plays on the natural and human desire to be nice. Nobody worth buying can be bought for the price of a lunch or a summer camp session for his child, but it's very hard for a decent person to refuse even to talk ("Just talk, Charlie, that's all I ask") to someone who's done him a favor. It's all the more difficult because that favor was most likely done out of a genuine desire to be nice as well as for the opportunity to get a return favor, and the official will sense this.

Taking an official to lunch or dinner is an innocent favor. But one begins to move away from innocence as the number of meals and the size of guest lists increase. When Tip O'Neill was Speaker of the House and accepted $7,000 worth of parties in his honor from Tongsun Park, the lobbyist for South Korea, it was wrong in two ways: First, the monetary value of the parties was far from minimal; second, his acceptance signaled to other congressmen that O'Neill and Park were friends, increasing Park's influence with them.

When Neil Bush was being investigated for his role in the Silverado Savings and Loan scandal, Lud Ashley provided free advice and raised money for the president's son.

This certainly did not injure the White House standing of Ashley's client, The Association of Bank Holding Companies which includes the nation's largest banks. Unfortunately for the public interest and the cause of justice, Ashley's assistance also helped Neil Bush escape significant punishment for his part in the scandal.

Other common examples of not-so-innocent favors include free trips to hunting lodges and conventions in places like Honolulu and free flights on private planes. During the eighties, for example, Senator Robert Dole paid the equivalent of only one first-class airfare each time he used chartered corporate jets belonging to General Mills, Warner-Lambert, and Metropolitan Life. There may have been no quid pro quo but Dole did appear to repay U.S. Tobacco Corporation for the use of its Gulfstream jet by supporting the tobacco subsidy program and opposing higher taxes on tobacco products.

When Al Ullman was chairman of the powerful House Ways and Means Committee, he received the following invitation from Jack Valenti, president of the Motion Picture Association of America (and who had once been an aide to Lyndon Johnson; the MPAA hired him as a favor to LBJ):

"Charles Bludhorn [chairman of Gulf and Western, which owns Paramount Pictures] and I are eager for you and your wife to join us and a few others for what I think will be a spectacular evening. Charlie will "premiere" the remarkable new film "Godfather II," at his home in New York City on Saturday evening, December 7. The evening will begin at 6:30 with cocktails, then the movie and dinner to follow. . . . A Gulfstream II will pick up and return you."

Valenti has since realized that he doesn't need the expensive jet trip to New York. He simply invites the influentials to MPAA's ornate Washington headquarters for an evening of food, drink, and a movie that the average man won't see for weeks or months. Valenti's guests are grateful not only for the evening but for the certification that the invitation gives to their reputation as influentials. All of this begets, in the words of the *Washington Post*'s Charles Trueheart, "at least a returned phone call, a granted appointment and that all important benefit of the doubt." It also begets Valenti a salary that in 1992 is in the neighborhood of $750,000.

It is impossible to understand the reality of modern lobbying by looking for an explicit quid pro quo. Most likely, Bludhorn and Valenti wanted nothing specific from Ullman at that time. All they may have wanted was Ullman's gratitude for a memorable evening, which would ease their access when they did need him later.

There is another way of obtaining gratitude. Tommy Boggs, a Washington lawyer who lobbies on behalf of such clients as Chrysler, General Motors, and BCCI did some free lobbying for the Carter administration on the Panama Canal treaty and SALT II. Such activity, needless to say, created a receptive climate for Boggs when his paying clients needed help at the White House. "I work with him all the time," said Anne Wexler, an assistant to President Carter. "If he comes in on behalf of a client, it's my responsibility to put him [in touch] with someone he needs."

Robert Gray, a prominent Republican lobbyist, gave free public relations advice to such Reagan administration figures as Ed Meese, James Watt, Anne Gorsuch, and Larry Speakes. "I always ask," Gray said, "if I can do anything to help." Craig Fuller, who was chief of George Bush's presidential campaign staff and then went into public relations in Washington, provided similar free advice to the Bush administration, as did other Republican lobbyists such as Sheila Tate, Ken Duberstein, and Charlie Black.

But these more subtle ways of winning access have not entirely displaced the direct cash payment. Although outright bribery is generally frowned on, something close to it was quite common in the seventies and eighties: the paid speaking engagement. Organizations would invite a representative or a senator to speak. The members would chat with him before he went onstage, share refreshments after the speech, and then present him with a check, which was delicately described as an "honorarium." This certainly did not tend to make him hostile to their interests.

Congress finally outlawed speaking honoraria in the early nineties. But it's still possible for an organization to fly a congressman and spouse to, say, Honolulu for a speech for which there will be no pay, but the couple will be wined and dined and have all their other expenses paid. If the organization has a lot of powerful or wealthy members who might help the congressman get reelected through their influence or contributions, the speaking engagement is even more of a favor to the congressman for which he will be indebted to the organization.

Next to the speaking engagement, the nearest legal equivalent to the straight cash bribe is the campaign contribution. It does not have to be very large. Indeed, the more conscientious the congressman, the more likely he is to be troubled by taking large contributions from a lobbyist and voting for the lobby on a pending bill. This explains why, except for especially greedy legislators such as the Keating Five and except in the larger states, where the amounts tend to be higher, the accepted "price" of access is $500 to $1,000 for congressmen and $2,000 for senators—not enough to be suspicious, but enough to help the campaign.

Lobbyists not only make contributions themselves but solicit them from others. Tommy Boggs is said to have raised funds for more Democratic candidates than anyone in Washington. Robert McCandless, a member of the Democratic National Committee's finance council, said of Boggs, "He has the ability to convince clients and his friends of their need to contribute. . . . You've got to be able to tell your clients that if they are going to do business in this town, they'd better make certain contributions to the party in power and to key people on the Hill." The American Medical Association has followed that advice perhaps better than any other lobbying group. Certainly it spends more.

For many organizations, the campaign contribution is a straightforward purchase of access rather than a commit-

ment to a candidate or his political philosophy. Contributions are made to important congressmen across the political spectrum, and it is not at all uncommon for contributions
to be made to both sides in the same political contest, just
to be safe.

One congressman told the *Wall Street Journal*: "Getting
elected to Congress is a painful ordeal. When you come out
of the cauldron you're extremely grateful to those who
helped you financially or with votes. Certainly the donors
want influence, they want to be able to come in any time
and have you listen. Of course you'll take a longer look at
their problems. If it doesn't violate your principles, you'll
try to lean their way, especially on an issue that doesn't
involve a lot of other people." Notice that the congressman
referred to "those who helped you financially or with votes."
Votes can be appreciated more than any amount of money,
especially if they can be produced or denied in significant
blocs. This is why lobbies with lots of members, like the
National Rifle Association or the National Education Association, wield enormous power.

Corporations can use their stockholders as the AFL-CIO
has used its members, but they have not often done so, with
one notable exception. They are taking full advantage of
legislation enacted in the seventies permitting managerial
employees to form political action committees (PACs)
through which they can make campaign contributions and
serve as campaign workers. These committees were pioneered by labor unions but have turned out to be a more
powerful tool for corporations. The PACs target powerful
politicians in making contributions. Thus in a fifteen-month
period in 1989–90, Senator J. Bennett Johnston collected
$236,500 from oil, gas, utility, and other energy groups.
Johnston is chairman of the Senate Energy Committee.

Pro-Israel PACs reward Israel's friends and punish those
who deviate. In that same 1989–90 period, Senator Paul
Simon, a faithful friend, got $122,651 from pro-Israel PACs.
The fate of the man he succeeded in the Senate, Charles

Percy, illustrates what happens to those who waver in their support for Israel. After a trip to the Middle East in the seventies, Percy, previously considered to be an uncritical supporter of Israel, told a reporter, "Israel and its leadership, for whom I have a high regard, cannot count on the United States in the future just to write a blank check." He said he thought Israel had missed opportunities to negotiate and called Yasser Arafat "more moderate, relatively speaking, than other extremists." What Percy may not have realized is that the fifty-thousand members of the American Israel Public Affairs Committee are listed on computer by congressional district so they can be immediately mobilized to write their congressmen when issues concerning Israel arise.

Columnist Tom Braden obtained a memorandum to Percy written by one of his staff members about what happened during the next week: "We have received 2,200 telegrams and 4,000 letters in response to your Mideast statements. . . . They run 95 percent against. As you might imagine, the majority of hostile mail comes from various Jewish communities in Chicago. They threaten to withhold their votes and support for any future endeavors."

In 1990, when automakers were faced with a fuel efficiency bill that they didn't like but that seemed to have a lot of support, they hired Jack Bonner, one of a new breed of grass-roots lobbyists. Since greater fuel efficiency would lead to smaller cars, Bonner tried to identify a large group of people spread through every congressional district that would not want smaller cars. His answer: the handicapped. He was able to generate thousands of letters from people all over the country who felt they needed large cars—enough letters to kill the proposed legislation.

For more than a hundred years the federal government was the biggest employer in the District of Columbia. But in 1979 it was surpassed by the "service" sector, which includes the law and public relations firms and the trade associations where paid lobbyists work. The rise of these organizations reflects the trend toward special-interest politics that has accompanied the decline of the political party. Party loyalty used to be a powerful force in determining legislative action. In his book *Wheeling and Dealing*, Bobby Baker tells of the time in the fifties when his boss, Lyndon Johnson, then minority leader of the Senate, managed to get a unanimous Democratic vote for repeal of the Taft-Hartley Act by appealing to party loyalty. Today, with party loyalty replaced by identification with interest groups, such a vote would be split between prolabor and probusiness senators. Power has been transferred from party to lobby.

The most startling example of how that power works is the story of Anna Chennault and the 1968 election. Madame Chennault was a lobbyist for the South Vietnamese government who became convinced, through assurances from the Nixon camp, that South Vietnam would do better if Nixon rather than his Democratic opponent, Hubert Humphrey, were to win the U.S. presidential election. In the final days of the campaign, precisely when Humphrey was overtaking Nixon in the polls and a peace agreement between the United States and North Vietnam—an agreement that would surely have accelerated Humphrey's momentum— seemed imminent, Madame Chennault persuaded the South Vietnamese to torpedo the peace talks. Nixon won the election.

What Madame Chennault did to Hubert Humphrey should teach every politician that if a lobbyist thinks Senator A will do a better job for his cause than Senator B, the lobbyist just might decide to arrange for Senator B's defeat (recall the case of Senators Simon and Percy). This is the threat that every lobbyist—at least, every lobbyist who commands a lot of money or a lot of votes—holds over the head of every elected official. The threat is seldom acted on, however. The lobbyist knows that if he should fail to defeat Senator B, the good senator will thereafter actively oppose whatever cause the lobbyist supports. So the best lobbyists make a point of never showing anger when they fail to persuade. Says Representative J. J. Pickle of Tommy Boggs, "I've never seen him put on a fuss when he loses. He lives on for the next day."

Like every really smart lobbyist, Boggs knows the importance of being subtle and of keeping a low profile. He avoids publicity because he knows it is the lobbyist's main enemy. Remember the case of Judge Walsh and Richard Kleindienst? Judge Walsh's lobbying for ITT, the perfect embodiment of these lessons, worked. But at the same time, ITT had another Washington lobbyist, Dita Beard, who had pledged $200,000 to help pay for the 1972 Republican convention. As she wrote her superiors about this gift: "If it gets too much publicity, you can believe our negotiations with Justice will wind up shot down. John Mitchell [then attorney general] is definitely helping but can't let it be known." The memo was leaked, sabotaging Beard's plot. It was Judge Walsh, using the network, who successfully carried ITT's water.

The network is the real secret. When Ellen Proxmire gave a surprise birthday party for her husband, William, when he was chairman of the Senate Banking Committee, guess where she gave it. Why, at Tommy Boggs's house, of course.

3.

THE
BUREAUCRACY

There is a permanent government in Washington that consists of people whose power does not depend on election results. It includes the courts, the military, and the foreign services as well as those two unofficial but powerful branches we have just examined, the press and lobbies. But the largest part of the permanent government is the bureaucracy, which has about three million federal civilian employees. Six times that number are funded by taxpayers as employees of state, county, and municipal governments or as members of the military. Millions more work for government contractors.

With so many of our citizens directly or indirectly working for government, it is not surprising that the bureaucratic presence is increasingly dominant in our lives. You experience it when you stand in line to get a driver's license, when you try to pry loose your aunt's overdue social security check, when you start to pay your taxes and realize you have to pay even more to hire someone to prepare your return.

Some bureaucrats do essential work. Air traffic controllers, Forest Service fire fighters, nurses at the Veterans'

Administration hospitals, and researchers seeking a cure for cancer or protecting you from dangerous drugs all perform vital functions that tangibly affect our daily lives.

But for every one of these obviously useful civil servants there is a government employee whose contribution to the public interest is less clear—the five thousand personnel managers and fifteen hundred public information and public relations specialists who were working for the Pentagon as recently as 1991, for example, or employees with such titles (all of them real) as Planning Analyst, Schemes Routing Specialist, Manager of Creative Services, Social Priorities Specialist, Suggestions Awards Administrator, Fringe Benefit Specialist, and Confidential Assistant to the Confidential Assistant. These bureaucrats have the better-paying jobs and usually work in the District of Columbia. I first encountered them when I moved to Washington from West Virginia in 1961. At that time I was a fervent believer in the civil service system. In the late fifties, while working on the staff of the West Virginia legislature, I drafted a bill designed to transform a patronage-riddled personnel system into a service based on merit that offered genuine career protection for state employees. My determination to get the bill enacted into law was one of the reasons I ran for a seat in the legislature in the next election, and it was a proud day in my life when the bill, bearing my name, was passed in the following session.

Then I came to Washington. Having seen the evils of having too many political hacks, I was now exposed to the evils of having too many planning analysts. The old West Virginia system was characterized by too much corruption and too little continuity; the Washington system was characterized by too much defensiveness and too little courage.

Certainly not all bureaucrats are defensive cowards. And of course in many clerical jobs courage or openness is irrelevant. But as people begin to climb the administrative ladder, a dominant personality type emerges—or perhaps certain elements in the personality come to dominate as a civil servant gets promoted. Either way, an excess of caution is one of the primary characteristics. It is ironic that a system intended to protect the courageous and outspoken has attracted people who rarely need protection on those counts. Instead, they are looking for protection against anything that could disturb their quiet but steady progress up the career ladder.

When did the bureaucracy turn into the lethargic, self-protective monster it is today? It became monstrous in size between 1933 and 1945, when it grew from five hundred thousand employees to three and a half million, but during those years it was inspired by the challenge of fighting the Depression and winning the war—and by an exciting leader, Franklin D. Roosevelt. The trend toward lethargy and self-protection, it seems to me, began with the end of the war and the death of FDR in 1945. Truman may be fondly remembered today, but in the late forties he was not perceived as an exciting or challenging leader by federal workers. The loyalty program he established in 1947 was the first step toward making them value caution and keeping out of trouble. Then came the attack from Congress, from William Jenner and Joseph McCarthy, from the "who lost China" mob. In 1952 the defeat of Adlai Stevenson, who as a candidate seemed to reawaken the idealism that had been dormant under Truman, was the final blow. The result was a near-total preoccupation with self-protection—a sense that the people at the top didn't share the civil servant's goals and didn't understand or care about his ideas unless the ideas were Red, which meant that he would be fired.

Any ardor that may have flared under John Kennedy or in the first years of Johnson's Great Society was snuffed out by Vietnam, so that by the early seventies the bureaucrat was firmly set in the defensive ways that persist today—and were in fact exacerbated by the Reagan administration's hostility toward government agencies outside the area of national security. He doesn't want his performance to be evaluated because, although it might bring praise and more rapid advancement, it might also bring an irrational inquiry into his political philosophy or the discovery that his performance has been less than superb. So whenever evaluation is attempted, he and his colleagues, allied in this cause as they are in no other, turn it into a joke. More than 99 percent of eligible federal employees got annual merit salary increases ("step" raises) throughout the seventies and eighties, in 1990, and in 1991—in other words, right up to the press date for this book. According to an article in the *Washington Post* in 1991, a civil servant's chances of being fired for poor performance are one in forty-three hundred.

Because his performance will not be evaluated, at least in any serious way, the civil servant knows that the only way he can lose his job is through a budget cut that affects his program. Therefore, since his survival depends on avoiding such cuts, it is in his interest to hide unhappy truths about his agency's performance from potential troublemakers such as the Office of Management and Budget, which determines the president's budget recommendations to Congress; the General Accounting Office, which can audit the agency's performance and say it doesn't deserve what it is getting; and Congress itself, which has the final word on how much money the agency will get.

"No activity in a government agency is given as high a priority as securing and enlarging its budget," Leonard Reed, a writer and former bureaucrat, has said. "Bureaucrats almost invariably believe in the function their agency exists to perform, whether it is providing information to farmers or preserving the national forests. A new bureaucracy, the darling of the administration that establishes it, has a missionary zeal about its function. As a bureaucracy ages, it loses glamour and finds itself expending an increasing share of its energy on obtaining funds. . . .

"Gradually a hierarchy of administrative officers, executive officers, budget officers, congressional liaison officers, and public information officers grows up, almost the sole purpose of which is fund-wheedling. Since there is a certain logic to the proposition that without money an agency can't function, the bureaucrat . . . finds nothing wrong with spending more and more of his time and attention aiding the quest for more money, much of which is now needed to support the large money-raising apparatus that has grown up in the agency."

The effort to justify its budget often affects the way an agency does the job it was created to do. In 1974, the Internal Revenue Service began to single out middle-income taxpayers, who historically have the best record of paying their taxes honestly, for a disproportionately large share of audits. Why? Congress had granted the IRS more auditors on the condition that they be used to increase the number of audits performed during the 1974 fiscal year. The IRS chose to perform middle-income audits because they are quicker to do than, say, a full-dress study of Mobil Oil. But at least back then it was doing audits. By 1990, after the triumph of the Reagan revolution, it was auditing only ninety-seven of every ten thousand returns, the lowest number in IRS history.

One of the most notorious results of the fear of budget cuts is the end-of-the-year spending spree—remember, the fact of bureaucratic life the entire staff at the *Washington Post* seemingly hadn't noticed. It was a traditional rite of spring in Washington until a few years ago, when the end of the fiscal year was changed from June 30 to September 30. Now the season—harvest time—couldn't be more appropriate, and the ritual remains otherwise unchanged. As the midnight hour of the last day of September approaches, each agency desperately tries to use up all its appropriated funds for the year so it won't appear to have been overbudgeted.

Several years ago Senator William Proxmire got hold of a memo sent by Admiral Elmo Zumwalt, then chief of naval operations, to his key subordinates, urging them to spend $400 million quickly before the fiscal year ended. When Proxmire held hearings on the memo and on the navy's efforts to get rid of the money by paying high claims to shipping contractors, Admiral Isaac Kidd, chief of the naval materiel command, explained: "We must . . . commit those funds within the prescribed period in order not to be put in a position of disadvantage later on by someone being able to say, "Well, you asked for money, but you did not spend it, so we are going to take it away or cut your budget next year.'"

How did Admiral Kidd meet this crisis? "We have gone with teams of competent contract people from Washington to outlying field activities to look over their books with them . . . to see in what areas there is susceptibility to improved capability to commit funds." As every taxpayer knows, there is never a shortage of that susceptibility.

Yet there are times when bureaucracies have turned down offers of money. When the Federal Energy Regulatory Commission solicited bids in 1990 for transcribing its hearings, three companies offered to do the job for free. The reason was that because so many rich oil and gas companies want copies, the transcriber can make money just by selling copies of the transcripts. One company, however, went even further, offering to pay the FERC $1.25 million for the privilege of transcribing the hearings.

So the FERC leapt in the air with delight and accepted the offer? No. James E. Thompson, the FERC's procurement director, said the money wouldn't do the FERC any good. By law, he explained to Dale Russakoff of the *Washington Post*, the money would have to go into the U.S. Treasury instead of helping to increase the budget of the FERC. The fact that it *would* help the Treasury and thereby help all American citizens is something the Thompsons of the civil service seldom stop to think about.

In its annual struggle to protect or enlarge its budget, a government agency has a decisive advantage over its natural enemy, the Office of Management and Budget, which appraises budget requests. The OMB might assign six or seven employees to size up a cabinet ᵓartment's budget, but the department will have 450 or 500 budget people whose job is to keep the OMB from finding out the truth. The agency may ask for four or five times what it needs for a program, confident that the OMB can't possibly track down all the overestimates and thus ensuring that the final figure that emerges will be satisfactory.

Sometimes agencies do just the opposite: They underestimate their funding needs. They do so, however, only for popular programs which require fixed payments to qualified recipients. If the program runs short of money during the fiscal year, Congress must pass what is called a supplemental appropriation to take care of the shortfall, or face a lot of angry constituents. The clever bureaucrat understands this. If, for instance, OMB says that a total of $9 billion is available for all activities of the Department of Agriculture, he might purposely underestimate the share of a price support program with broad support among farmers, using some (or all) of it to fatten the appropriations for other agricultural programs instead, then go back to Congress later in the year to get the money to bail out price supports.

If OMB sees through all these tricks, there is yet another device the bureaucrat can try—offering the OMB investigator a higher salary to come work for the agency. When this is done by a private government contractor, the impropriety is obvious. But it has been done within the government—rarely, it is true, but still, the subtle hint of even the possibility of such employment has often been enough to restrain OMB analysts from excessive zealousness.

One more budget-protecting ploy often works even when the OMB recognizes it. I call it the Firemen First Principle. The basic idea is that, when faced with a budget cut, the bureaucrat translates it into bad news for members of Congress who are powerful enough to restore the amount eliminated. In other words, he chops where it will hurt constituents the most, not the least. At the local government level, this is most often done by threatening reductions in fire and police protection. At the federal level, Amtrak provided this example of how to play the game: Once when it was threatened with a budget cut, it immediately announced that it would have to drop the following routes:

• San Francisco–Bakersfield, running through Stockton, the hometown of the chairman of the House Appropriations Transportation Subcommittee;

• St. Louis–Laredo, running through Little Rock, Arkansas, the hometown of the chairman of the Senate Appropriations Committee; and

• Chicago–Seattle, running through the hometowns of the Senate majority leader and of the chairman of the Senate Commerce Committee.

And in a triumphant stroke that netted four birds with one roadbed, Amtrak threatened to cut a route from Norfolk to Chicago that ran through the home states of the chairman of the Senate Appropriations Transportation Subcommittee, the chairman of the Senate Commerce Surface Transportation Subcommittee, the chairman of the House Commerce Committee, and of Robert Byrd of West Virginia, then the Senate majority whip.

The effectiveness of Amtrak's approach is suggested by a story about Byrd's response that appeared in the *Charleston Gazette* a few days after the announcement, under the headline CONTINUED RAIL SERVICE BYRD'S AIM:

"Senator Robert C. Byrd, D-W.Va., has announced that he intends to make an effort today to assure continued rail passenger service for West Virginia. Byrd, a member of the Senate Appropriations Committee, said he will 'Either introduce an amendment providing sufficient funds to continue the West Virginia route or try to get language adopted which would guarantee funding for the route for Amtrak.'"

In the Amtrak case, the bureaucrat's budget-cutting enemy was OMB. It can sometimes be a frugal superior in the bureaucrat's own department, but the trick still works. If, for example, a secretary of defense from South Carolina suggests eliminating useless military bases to save money, the navy's bureaucrats will promptly respond with a list of expendable bases that is headed by the Charleston Navy Yard.

The bureaucrat will almost always say that a budget cut is sure to result in the loss of jobs. The directly threatened employees will then write their congressman, who will almost certainly vote to restore the funds since no one will have written him in support of the cut.

There is another aspect of the bureaucrat's concern about the loss of others' jobs. He knows he can't be a commander without troops to command. During much of the seventies and eighties the navy deprived its fleet of essential maintenance while continuing to spend billions on superfluous supercarriers and to trade small Polaris submarines for giant Tridents. The reason was that the more big ships with big crews there are, the more admirals are needed.

The same principle applies to the civil service, where rank is determined in part by the number of employees one supervises. Thus a threat to reduce the number of a bureaucrat's employees is a challenge not merely to his ego, but also to his position and income.

When menaced with a budget cut, the clever bureaucrat realizes that the public will support his valiant fight against the reduction only if essential services are endangered. Concentrated in the headquarters for bureaucracies of the New York City and District of Columbia school systems, for example, are some of the most prodigious do-nothing time-servers of the modern era. But until the budget crunches of the early nineties, no administrator ever threatened to fire them. They are the fat, and it would have damaged his cause even to admit their existence. Instead the administrator threatens a loss of muscle—essential teachers. Similarly, the army, when faced with a budget cut, never points the finger at desk-bound lieutenant colonels. The would-be victims are invariably combat troops. This practice is particularly unfortunate because in government, as in human beings, fat tends to concentrate at the middle levels, where planning analysts and deputy assistant administrators spend their days writing memoranda and attending meetings.

Memoranda and meetings are where the survival and make-believe principles merge. Bureaucrats write memoranda both because they appear to be busy when they are writing and because the memos, once written, immediately become proof that they were busy. They attend meetings for the same reason. Indeed, most bureaucrats make a big production of rushing off to meetings; meaningful action is seldom taken but the appearance of action is satisfied by the fact that the meeting was held. (Sometimes, attending a meeting is a prudent precaution against the possibility that bureaucratic enemies might use the occasion to cut your budget or lower your personnel ceiling.)

I have recently had extensive dealings with an organization whose members seem to spend almost all their time in meetings, leaving them only a few minutes a day to actually do something. Such organizations are common in government and among corporations whose previous leadership has built enough cash flow to spare present employees from bottom-line worries. The essential futility of these meetings is indicated by a review of studies on brainstorming reported by the *New York Times* in 1988 which found that "on average brainstorming groups [meaning meetings] did less well than the same number of people pooling ideas they came up with on their own." In the meetings, participants are usually preoccupied with impressing one another—and their superiors. The problem is that everyone tends to forget about impressing the world with the organization's real accomplishments. A private company will ultimately pay the penalty as cash flow dries up, but in government the meetings go on and on and on and on.

The Peters Principle—take care to distinguish it from the less persuasive Peter Principle—provides that organizations cease to function effectively when employees spend more than 15.8 percent of their time attending meetings or writing memoranda. When I was in the Peace Corps, I

learned that the employees of a young and vigorous organization are filled with urgency and excitement about what
they are doing. They can't bear to waste time attending
formal meetings or fussing over the wording of a memo.
They communicate by phone, by shouting across the room,
or by catching one another in the hallway. It is not until
they become more concerned with the appearance of action
than with action itself that they begin to favor meetings. If
you can go to a meeting, it appears you are doing something.
Indeed, you can even seem breathlessly busy as you pull on
your coat and rush off, shouting over your shoulder, "Hold
the phone calls, Mrs. Jones, I've got to make that two o'clock
meeting in Smithers's office."

Naturally, the most favored meetings are those that involve travel. Here's an example from the travel records of
the District of Columbia's Departments of Human Resources and Education for one fiscal year. The Department
of Human Resources sent fifteen employees to San Francisco
for the annual meeting of the American Public Health
Association and nine employees to Honolulu to attend a
convention of the American Psychiatric Association. It also
sent Raymond Standard, administrator of the Community
Health and Hospitals Administration, to Aspen, Colorado,
for thirty-nine days to attend a session entitled "Effective
Strategies for Change." But his record was eclipsed by Dr.
Jefferson McAlpine, administrator for the Mental Health
Administration, who managed to stay on the road for fifty-
one days. "If the same meeting that took place in Honolulu
had been held in Baltimore," Dr. McAlpine told a reporter,
"there would have been no question on it." The trouble is
that the meeting is seldom in Baltimore.

In fact, there were only three individual trips to Balti-
more and a total of seventy-four trips to San Francisco,
Honolulu, Montreal, San Diego, Disneyland, St. Thomas,
Quebec, Atlantic City, Williamsburg, Aspen, White Sulphur
Springs, Miami, Tampa, and New Orleans. On group trips,
Baltimore struck out completely; meanwhile, groups rang-

ing in size from two to twenty-five managed to get to Squaw
Valley, Ocean City, Denver, San Francisco, Virginia Beach,
Atlantic City, Disneyland, Miami, New Orleans, San Juan,
and Honolulu.

Some agencies have their own aircraft for the travel convenience of bureaucrats. The Army Corps of Engineers, for
example, owns three planes, including a fourteen-passenger
executive jet. A recent study of the corps's flights by the
Army Audit Agency concluded that "virtually all the flights
were for routine matters and could have been accomplished
with commercial aircraft." If the corps sold its aircraft it
would gain $6.4 million for the Treasury, and if it used
regular airlines it would save $1 million more in travel
costs. The army, by the way, has an interesting definition
of routine. One of the corps's planes carried wives of corps
employees to a conference of the International Association
of Navigational Congresses in Helsinki. The wives' itiner-
ary, according to the Associated Press, "included sightseeing, a fashion show, and visits to an old cottage and a candy
factory."

The bureaucrat's yearning to see the world is so powerful
that even officials of agencies with exclusively domestic
responsibilities manage to find conferences and meetings to
attend abroad at taxpayers' expense. Thus Daniel Oliver of
the Federal Trade Commission managed to spend ninety-
five days abroad in the period 1986–88, visiting such cities
as Nassau, Geneva, Berlin, Tokyo, and that hotbed of antitrust activity, Acapulco.

What would happen if we called the bureaucrat's bluff
and cut his budget? Unless he thinks we know about the
real fat, about those trips to Acapulco, he may—to preserve
his credibility—actually fire essential employees. We could
end up with a government run by planning analysts and
friends of senators under whose rule trains would always
run from San Francisco to Bakersfield via Stockton.

To cut fat and not muscle out of the federal budget, four

interrelated inflations need to be looked at: inflated pay, inflated job descriptions, inflated grades, and inflated slots.

The last is easiest to explain: Suppose the country were being overrun by Albanian moths. The Department of Agriculture would ask the Civil Service Commission for authority to establish positions for, say, two hundred Albanian Moth Control Officers. Because of the emergency, the authority would be granted and Agriculture would have two hundred new slots. Suppose the Albanian moth were then brought under control. Would the slots be abolished? Certainly not. Now you understand slot inflation.

Then there is grade inflation, sometimes called grade creep. In one study the Civil Service Commission—hardly the system's severest critic—found that 150,000 workers had been overgraded, meaning their rank was higher than the level of their actual work required. In 1955, 8.2 percent of federal workers were in the upper middle class of the civil service, grades GS-12 through GS-15. Today the figure is 28.9 percent. Grade creep means too many chiefs and too few Indians, too many supervisors and too few people to do the work.

Related to grade inflation is payroll inflation. Although some technical and professional employees are underpaid— how can we ever adequately compensate the air traffic controller who skillfully handles nervewracking rush hours at JFK—many civil servants are paid too much for the jobs they do. In 1992, the average civil servant earns $6,000 more than the average American makes—$14,000 more if the civil servant happens to be among the privileged group that works inside the Capital Beltway. GS-15s, many of whom have responsibilities comparable to those of the manager of a Safeway store, make as much as $83,502 per year, and they are only at the top of the middle grades. Above them are the cream of the career bureaucrats, the members of the Senior Executive Service, whose salaries range from $90,000 to $112,100.

If government jobs paid as poorly as bureaucrats say they do, wouldn't there be a shortage of applicants and wouldn't bureaucrats be resigning in droves to accept better-paying jobs in private industry? Neither, of course, is happening. In Washington, an average of 300,000 people a year seek government jobs. There are few positions to fill, however: Only 1 percent of those applicants ever find an administrative job—and I mean any administrative job.

Behind the inflated grades and pay lies the fourth kind of inflation: the inflated job description, the document by which the civil service system determines rank and salary. "Anybody who has ever worked in a government agency," writes Leonard Reed, "knows that job descriptions will endow a file clerk with responsibilities before which a graduate of the Harvard Business School would quail." In even the smallest bureaucratic unit you will find at least one person skilled in writing job descriptions, who can turn typists into "word processors" and elevator operators into "vertical vehicle controllers." Those ten-dollar words produce thousand-dollar raises.

Inflation in grade means inflation in space as well. A GS-6 gets sixty square feet of office space, while a GS-16 gets three hundred square feet. It's an indication of the extent of grade inflation that the amount of office space for each civilian government employee has gone up 66 percent since 1965.

Reducing all this inflation is not easy. Government employees can be fired by a process called RIF (reduction in force) if their agency's budget has been cut. But a RIF endangers the government's efficiency because employees are retained or dismissed on the basis of seniority, not ability. The idiotic result of this policy was illustrated in 1991 when Cathy Nelson, who had just been named Minnesota's Teacher of the Year, was laid off because of lack of seniority. The Reagan administration struck a demoralizing blow to the morale of the best civil servants when it used RIF to dismiss several thousand of the young without regard to how capable they were, while retaining senior employees' services without regard to how dull or incompetent *they* were. But the administration had no choice of method of firing because over the years civil servants have managed to get regulations and court rulings that make it next to impossible to fire them any other way. As one observed, "We're all like headless nails down here—once you get us in, you can't get us out."

Just how hard it is is indicated by the case of Clarence Ferguson, an employee of the National Marine Fisheries Service in St. Petersburg, Florida. Ferguson, according to the *St. Petersburg Times*, drank a pint of gin a day. During the years 1980–83 he missed 389 days of work. Finally he was fired. Now a federal judge has given him the right to get his job back and has awarded him $150,000 in back pay. The judge reasoned that all federal agencies should make reasonable accommodation for their "handicapped" workers, including alcohol and drug addicts.

An alcoholic who misses 389 days of work deserves our sympathy and our help in overcoming his addiction, but he does not deserve a government job. The only standard that should govern the retention of employees is performance— performance that demonstrates competence and dedication to the public interest.

One high-level bureaucrat claims that showing cause for firing, as the law requires, can take up to 50 percent of the bureaucrat's working time for a period that may run from six to eighteen months. The executive must keep a diary of the employee's indiscretions (tardiness, mistakes, goofing off, flubbed assignments) before filing a complaint is possible. Protected by a maze of regulations and limitations and often defended by lawyers from government employees' unions, a civil servant threatened with firing can drag a hearing out for months or even years. Eventually the boss may begin to feel he is himself on trial: His own reputation may suffer as his colleagues and superiors accuse him of creating friction. At higher levels of government, as Leonard Reed notes, "harmony is valued well above function."

The result is a bureaucracy that is not only overstaffed but overstaffed with unproductive employees, employees who know that the government's rate of discharge for inefficiency is only one-seventh of 1 percent. Translated to a small business with ten employees, that's a rate of firing one person every seventy years.

What would happen if there were a dramatic reduction in the number of government employees—cutting it in half, say, as Scott Shuger recommended in an article in *The Washington Monthly* in 1990? There is no conclusive evidence on this point, but scattered returns are suggestive. Have you noticed any difference in the service you get from Washington bureaucrats during the last two weeks of December? Probably not, but did you know that in recent years absenteeism among Washington federal employees during that time has run as high as 60 percent?

Also revealing is the discovery made by the municipal government of the District of Columbia that the productivity of its trash collection crews increased when the crews were reduced from four men to three. And then there was the experience of the late Ellis O. Briggs when he was ambassador to Czechoslovakia. The Czechs became angry at the United States for one thing or another and ordered two-thirds of the American embassy staff sent home. Briggs found the stripped-down embassy the most efficient he'd ever known.

Probably the greatest obstacle to reform of the civil service is that most people think it is better to have a system based on merit hiring than one based on political patronage. But the fact is that getting a government job has only the most modest relation to merit. Veterans get five free points added to their civil service exam score; disabled veterans get an extra ten. For nonveterans the trick is to know someone inside the agency. People already in the system are the first to know about a job opening, and knowing both the applicant and the job, they can tailor the job description to fit the person they want to hire. So the civil service is a patronage ring based not on politics but on friendship. Insiders call it the "buddy system."

Even at the height of Watergate, Gordon Freedman, formerly of the House Manpower and Civil Service Subcommittee, contended that the real saboteurs of the civil service concept are civil servants themselves. "Sure, some politicians get jobs for their friends," he said, "but you could put all the Nixon-referred people on the *Sequoia* [a small yacht used by Nixon] and it would still float. But if you put all the people involved in the buddy system on the carrier *Enterprise*, it would sink."

A decade later, in 1982, a similar conclusion was reached by a study conducted by the Merit System Protection Board called "Breaking Trust: Prohibited Personnel Practices in the Federal Service" which found that "most forms of political abuse—thought to be the greatest threat to the merit system—actually occur at insignificant levels of frequency." The most common abuse, the study reported, was the buddy system which was described as civil servants' "granting preferential treatment or access to people known by direct or indirect acquaintance, independent of those persons' merit relative to other competitors." And, another decade later, in 1991, a former director of the Office of Personnel Management wrote: "Unfortunately the old merit examination for government employment is dead. What replaced the merit system? The buddy system. With no examination—or what amounted to the same thing, the widely used credentials exams which do not differentiate very well, why not pick friends or relatives. The law forbids nepotism, but it does not forbid referring your child or spouse to another buddy who will hire the relative through the same exam that scores about everyone the same, and then request the relative by 'name' from the 'examination' score lists."

The result, the former director says, is that more than

"90 percent of the mid-to-upper level positions are filled by one employee requesting another by name."

The merit system is thus one of Washington's purest forms of make-believe. Average citizens think that these mid and upper level civil servants are promoted on the basis of rigorous written examinations when the credentials exam is in fact merely another civil servant evaluating a personnel file. They therefore blame not the buddy system but political patronage for government inefficiency.

Another reason behind the opposition to political patronage is the national disdain for politics and politicians. Philip Terzian expressed this attitude well when he wrote in the *New Republic* that "the pursuit of power is fundamentally a Philistine occupation, and it is not likely that a genuine intellectual, mindful of history and human nature, would find the transient glory of public affairs worth the trouble."

We have an inexplicable regard for people who are "above" politics. Among countless possible examples, Secretary of Defense James Forrestal was praised by the *New York Times* for being above politics when he didn't support Truman in the 1948 campaign, and both he and the *Times* were astonished when Truman proceeded to fire him. Forrestal was a Coriolanus. For him, being above politics really meant being above the mob. And this, I suspect, is the true attitude of most of the American elite.

It is widely assumed that a patronage system results in a government run by unqualified people. Let's take a look at that assumption. Why do political employees have to be unqualified? A politically appointed typist could be required to type the same number of words a minute as the civil service typist. Remember that merit appointment and promotion are not the reality in the present civil service; the system is only make-believe. Friendship has a lot more to do with hiring and advancement.

Isn't it possible that government jobs might best be filled by politicians who are interested in putting together an administration that will do a good enough job to get them reelected? The same principle applies to most of the decisions government employees make. Why shouldn't they be made on a partisan basis if the motive behind them is doing a good enough job to be reelected?

Instead of caring about doing a good job, far too many civil servants seem to be concerned primarily with their own comfort and convenience. Consider the case of Jerry M. Brown, medical coordinator for the Federal Emergency Management Agency, who left for vacation the day after the California earthquake in 1989. Why did Brown feel justified in leaving, especially since the agency's manpower resources had already been severely strained by Hurricane Hugo? Because he had purchased nonrefundable airline tickets.

Even high-level jobs have tended to be filled in recent years with people dedicated not to the success of the administration but rather to their own progress up the meritocratic ladder from one prestigious post to another that is even more impressive. They are so intent on getting ahead that they usually serve only a couple of years in any one job before moving on.

This is particularly true at the assistant secretary level. Since World War II the average assistant secretary has spent twenty-one months in the job. The result is particularly unfortunate because, since the cabinet secretary or agency head has to spend most of his time worrying about the White House, the press, and Congress and has little time for the affairs of his own department, the assistant secretary level is where the government is actually run.

The main advantage of the career civil service is continuity. When I worked at the Peace Corps in the sixties there was a five-year limit on employment. The policy brought a steady, stimulating infusion of new blood and resulted in a much more adventurous group of employees than would be attracted by the security of tenure. There was, however, a lack of continuity, and by the time I left the discussions at staff meetings had begun to sound like broken records. I heard problems wrangled over again and again as if they were brand new and the agency had no experience that would suggest their solution.

There is another reason for not doing away with civil service tenure completely. Occasionally, unwise or corrupt political decisions may threaten federal agencies, thus making it in the survival interest of the civil servants who work in them to blow the whistle on whatever wrongdoing is going on.

The role of the FBI and the CIA during the Watergate scandal shows how important the loyalty of the civil servant to his institution can be. When people in the White House wanted to contain the Watergate investigation, it was the civil servants who rebelled and leaked information to the press. Indeed, the Watergate stories of the FBI and CIA illustrate both the good and the bad sides of the civil servant's institutional loyalty: Both agencies showed an admirable, if only occasionial and self-preserving, willingness to stand up to political authority gone wrong, coupled with a mindless and equally self-preserving dedication to covering up their own sins.

So instead of abolishing the civil service, perhaps 50 percent of federal jobs, as they open up through normal attrition, should be filled with appointees who can be fired at any time. (This doesn't mean, of course, that we should keep all the present jobs and just change people; it's clear that besides the problem of untouchable incompetents, there's a problem of jobs that are useless no matter who's doing them. It's a particularly thorny situation, because at least part of almost every job is useful—in some cases it may be only 10 percent, but because the Albanian moth is seldom completely eradicated, it's rarely nothing at all.)

Being able to fire people is important because the civil service underwent a dramatic decline in quality during the 70s and 80s. At the end of that period a study by the Volcker Commission found that nearly ninety percent of college honor students never seriously consider working in government. Pat Ingraham, a professor of government who worked for the commission said: "I've talked with hundreds of line managers and administrators from practically every federal agency. And what I hear is the quality of new hires is just getting worse and worse." A report issued in 1988 by the Hudson Institute spoke of "a slowly emerging crisis of competence" in the federal government. The political scientist, James Q. Wilson, said the quality of the civil service has entered into "a death spiral."

A major reason for this decline was the hostility to government of the Nixon, Ford, Reagan and Bush administrations and the neglect of recruiting for the civil service that was the natural result of their attitude. Donald Devine, Reagan's director of the Office of Personnel Management, halted all recruiting by his agency. Terry Cutler, one of Devine's assistants, wrote in an op-ed piece for the *Wall Street Journal*:

"The government does not need top graduates, administrative offices staffed with MBAs from Wharton, or policy shops full of the best and brightest whatevers. Government's goal should not be employee excellence but employee sufficiency."

With sights set so low, it's little wonder that the administrations have left us with a lot of government employees who are insufficient. If we are going to revitalize the government we must be able to replace them with men and women who are both talented and committed.

The key to democratic politics is accountability. If you don't deliver the goods, the voters can throw you out. Remember that when the Post Office was political it worked. We got our mail promptly. It was delivered twice a day, packages arrived intact, and a stamp cost three cents. Today it costs ten times as much, but the service has gotten so bad that United Parcel Service and Federal Express have become rich filling the vacuum.

This pattern of declining service and rising prices did not keep the Postal Service from awarding nearly $20 million in bonuses to its top executives between 1988 and 1990, when the Postal Service not only was not making a profit but actually lost more than $1.4 billion. The rigorous standards used in evaluating the performance of these executives is suggested by the fact that, of all those who could have gotten bonuses, 97 percent received them. And during 1989, while they were eliminating Sunday collections at thousands of mailboxes, postal officials spent more than $6 million on conferences for themselves in such places as Scottsdale, Arizona; Naples, Florida; Marina del Rey, California; and Maui, Hawaii. At Scottsdale, $13,000 was spent on three pre-dinner drinking parties and $99 a person for just one dinner.

The reason the Post Office stopped working was that it became nonpolitical. When it worked, congressmen knew that if the postmasters they appointed didn't deliver the mail, the congressmen would be blamed by the voters. Now the congressmen can say that's out of their hands. And it is out of their hands. Congress has surrendered vast powers to independent federal agencies over which it and the president have little or no authority. Bureaucrats in such agencies feel beyond public control. Even when Congress or the president gives them an order, they find ways to subvert it.

The Library of Congress recently studied federal agencies' compliance with the Sunshine Act of 1976, which was supposed to open government up to the public. The study found that of a group of 1,003 government meetings listed in the *Federal Register*, 627 were either partially or completely closed to the public. One closed meeting was held by the Federal Reserve Board to consider the design of its furniture; it was closed on the grounds that "matters of a sensitive financial nature were being considered by the Board."

The military is a master of this kind of subversion. When the navy was ordered to conserve fuel during the energy crisis of the early seventies, it reported that it had reduced its ships' sailing time by 20 percent. What it actually did was redefine *sailing time* to exclude a ship's journey from port to the fleet at sea. When it was discovered that lunches served in the Pentagon's Army General Officers' Mess cost taxpayers an average of six times the prices the officers paid, the army announced reform: "Meal prices must be sufficient to cover operating expenses and food costs." Did the generals give up their bargain? Not on your life. They redefined *expenses* to exclude such items as stoves, utilities, and waiters' and cooks' salaries.

What is this if it is not make-believe? Laws are passed, orders are given, compliance seems to occur, but nothing changes. Bureaucrats don't like real change, only the appearance of change. That is why they are so fond of reorganization. Reorganization gives them something to do— redrawing charts, knocking down office walls—but nothing outside the agency, such as poverty or hunger or disease, is affected in the slightest. What does happen is that new jobs are created, almost always with higher grade classifications, which of course mean higher salaries for the reorganizers.

The reason bureaucrats like internal reorganization better than external action is easy to understand. Suppose you work in an antipoverty agency and you do your job so well that poverty is eradicated. Or suppose you work in the Department of Energy and the energy problem disappears. What will happen to you? The bureaucrat can figure that out. If he takes real action, if he's truly effective, he'll be out of work—he won't survive. If, on the other hand, his action is make-believe, poverty will not disappear, the energy problem will not be solved, and his job will be safe— he will survive. Now you understand the fundamental Washington equation:

$$Make\text{-}believe = Survival$$

4.

THE FOREIGN SERVICES

"Burns admired professional diplomats—men who were cool, collected, in control. . . . He saw himself as one of a dozen men in . . . an anteroom in a foreign chancellery (Belgrade? Helsinki?) conducting secret negotiations, ADC to a giant, Bohlen or Kennan, taking on the Russians by sheer force of logic and remorseless dialectic, arguing them back. . . . Forcing an agreement, and then a laconic cable to the Department. *Negotiations concluded*."

Thus Ward Just captures in his short story, "Burns," the life foreign service officers dream about but seldom lead.

It's not that their lives lack adventure. "A friend of ours," wrote Bill Keller and Ann Cooper in *The Washington Monthly*, "is a cultural officer in the foreign service. We see him occasionally on his holidays, and he always has terrific stories that fire up our sense of adventure—stories of crossing the Sahara with Bedouins, riding the White Nile steamer from Juba to Khartoum, dodging mortar fire in Lebanon."

What is missing is significant work. Those secret negotiations seldom take place. As Keller and Cooper note, their friend "never talks about the *work* he does, but we always assumed that this was just a diplomat's discretion in the presence of journalists. Once, however, at a Thanksgiving reunion of old friends, we asked him for a specific example of what it is, exactly, that a cultural officer does. There was a long, hesitant pause, and then he came up with one: he had once arranged the visit of an American bluegrass band to Kuwait."

In comparing the image of life in the foreign service with the reality at the U.S. embassy in Morocco, Keller and Cooper found:

"The international intrigue, the classified cables, the ringside seat at the unfolding of great events—this is the glamorous image of diplomacy, an image carefully nurtured by generations of State Department officials. Close up, the picture is very different, our experience suggests that on an overseas tour of duty the typical diplomat lives a life largely consumed by make-work, devoid of genuine responsibility, and contributing little to the advancement of America's interests abroad."

Drafting cables to be dispatched to Washington is one of the principal occupations of the foreign service officer in the field. The problem is that the cable, labored over long and lovingly by the field officer, is rarely read by the secretary of state, to whom it is addressed. Indeed, it is often not read by anyone other than the State Department desk officer for the country concerned and a few minor officials who need to pass the time but have no power to do anything in response to the cable.

As a result, many field officers become as desperate as the one my friend Stanley Meisler, who served from 1966 to 1990 as a foreign correspondent for the *Los Angeles Times*, encountered in his travels. The officer was so frustrated by the lack of reaction from Washington to his carefully crafted cables that he asked Meisler if he would mind reading them. What the FSO obviously craved was the knowledge that *someone* had read his work and valued it. The words he yearned to hear: "This is a masterpiece of concise reporting. Thanks to you I understand the situation in Botswana perfectly."

Why is the average citizen unaware of this problem? Probably because when the diplomat returns to this country he wants Mom and Dad and his friends back home to think he was performing tasks of the gravest importance while he was overseas. So why would he go around advertising that his work was largely ignored by his superiors?

In other words, the typical diplomat is much like his fellow government employee in Washington. His main activity is make-believe, and as we shall see, his main goal is survival.

The State Department is one of three sizable civilian bureaucracies involved in foreign affairs. (We will deal with the military in the next chapter.) Another, the supersecret National Security Agency, breaks other countries' codes. Then there are the military intelligence agencies and the Central Intelligence Agency as well as smaller organizations such as the Agency for International Development, the U.S. Information Agency, and the Peace Corps. This is not to mention minor contingents from the FBI, the Drug Enforcement Administration, the Departments of Agriculture and Commerce, and a few other agencies that manage to get a foot in our embassies' doors.

While the bureaucratic characteristics of these organizations are similar to those we have found in domestic agencies, some are unique to the area of foreign affairs—or can be found there in either larger or more dangerous doses.

One such characteristic is clientism. This is the tendency of our representatives to inflate the importance to the United States of the country in which they are serving. A dispassionate observer might expect that cabinet changes in Senegal or Sierra Leone are of little importance to us. But you can be sure that the members of the U.S. country team, which is what the group of senior representatives of the various American agencies in the foreign country is called, are dramatizing every development with cables to Washington marked TOP SECRET and EYES ONLY. Their reasoning is that if Washington thinks the country is important, it will think they are important, with a resulting rise in their prospects for the various promotions, raises, and honors they know in their hearts they so richly deserve.

Clientism can take another form: identification with the host country or with those currently in power there. Lyndon Johnson once complained that his ambassador to India, Chester Bowles, was really another ambassador *for* India, seemingly more interested in advocating India's cause than that of the United States. Throughout the seventies and eighties the most conspicuous victim of clientism was our ambassador to Japan, Mike Mansfield, who was almost completely blind to Japan's economic sins against the United States.

This kind of clientism can have a darker side: In 1969 Thomas Melady was our ambassador to Burundi, a small Central African country with a history of tribal bloodshed between the Tutsi, the dominant minority, and the Hutu, who made up 85 percent of the country's population but had been denied political and economic power. The Tutsi feared the United States would take sides with the oppressed Hutu, but Melady set about overcoming his clients' concerns. "He told them every chance he got," remembered one American official, "that the United States was absolutely impartial . . . that their relations were their own affair [doesn't this remind you of what American diplomats were saying to Saddam Hussein before August 1990 about his relations with Kuwait?] and he apparently got through to them." U.S.-Burundi relations were never better. Then in May 1973 the Tutsi murdered a quarter million Hutu.

Melady worried about reporting the genocide to Washington, afraid that the State Department would somehow "overreact" and destroy his carefully nurtured relationship. He arranged a letter to the Burundi government from several members of the diplomatic corps. "It was a low-key thing," one embassy staff member recalled, "saying we were concerned with their difficulties." Another remembered it as "tactful . . . it got no real response."

There is little doubt about Melady's motive. "He wouldn't sacrifice the relations he's built up," the source told Roger Morris, who described the episode in an article in *The Washington Monthly* several years ago. Ronald Reagan later rewarded Melady by giving him another ambassadorship and by making him assistant secretary of education.

In an attempt to avoid clientism, the State Department tries to move its employees from one post to another well before their roots grow too deep. Another motive is that no one wants to get stuck in out-of-the-way places such as Ougadougou for more than two or three years. This is the main reason for the frequent shifts of personnel that are characteristic of these agencies. If you've been in Ougadougou (it's the capital of Burkina Faso, West Africa), you're likely to get Paris, Rome, or Singapore next.

One result of these frequent transfers is that too few foreign service officers have the time or the motivation to learn the local language and culture of whatever country they happen to be assigned to. This problem was pointed out dramatically more than thirty years ago in a book called *The Ugly American*. Yet in Iran, at the time of the takeover of our embassy in Tehran in 1978, only one in ten of the foreign service officers stationed there was even minimally competent in Farsi, Iran's principal language. Of the 30 Americans serving in our consulate in Bombay in 1990, not one spoke the local language well enough to do more than take a taxi across town.

Only a handful of American universities teach Farsi. Not many more offer Arabic, whose crucial importance is even more evident. The result is that the State Department must subtract valuable years from the foreign service officer's working life for language instruction. And often the time allotted is too short for fluency.

Frequent transfers are also bad for institutional memory. Since there is a new staff every few years, no one can remember what happened more than a few years ago. William Paddock, who was writing a book about the effectiveness of American foreign assistance programs, returned to Guatemala to visit the Agency for International Development (AID) mission where he had worked nearly twenty years earlier. He talked to the mission's director, William Hinton about The Barcenas Projects:

Paddock: I understand Barcenas includes the forestry school the U.S. government helped establish ten years ago and later helped merge with the agricultural school there.

Hinton: I don't know anything about that. You must remember that I have been here only fifteen months. There is a lot about previous programs I don't know.

Paddock: Is any money going into the experiment station at Barcenas?

Hinton: What experiment station? There is no experiment station there in the sense any of us would think of one. It's a work farm for the Barcenas students. . . .

Paddock: I don't mean the school's farm, I mean the experiment station. When I worked here this station and the station at Chocola formed a major U.S. government effort. . . .

Hinton: I know nothing about it. I'm still learning.

Another basic truth about the foreign affairs bureaucracy was uncovered by Paddock when he asked Covey Oliver, then assistant secretary of state for Inter-American affairs, to select a successful project for Paddock to visit. Oliver recommended Los Brillantes in Guatemala, where he said AID was succeeding in helping Guatemalan farmers break the bonds of their dependence on a single crop, coffee, by supplying seedlings, advice, and loans to encourage the planting of rubber, citrus, and other crops. When Paddock reached Los Brillantes, "the place seemed dead." There was only one AID employee there. The loan money had run out. None of the farmers were planting rubber or citrus.

Why had Oliver thought the project a success? The foreign affairs bureaucracy, like bureaucracies in general, tends to gild the lily as information travels from the field to the home office. A project that is a disaster will be presented to top Washington officials as an outstanding success.

The reason for the lily-gilding is that subordinates want to please their superiors, which is also why subordinates don't speak up when their opinions might not be popular with the people at the top. William A. Bell, a former foreign service officer, tells these stories:

• In 1966, when the commitment of American ground forces in Vietnam took its greatest leap forward, criticism of U.S. policy became widespread among foreign service officers, or at least among those stationed in Washington. A number of young officers, some of whom had been privately expressing their misgivings, were called together for a briefing before setting out on campus recruiting trips. One of them asked the recruitment director what they should say to students who were interested in the foreign service but had qualms about the American role in Vietnam. The answer—in no uncertain terms: there was no place in the foreign service for persons who did not support the war. Not one of the young officers spoke up to disagree with the recruitment director.

• In 1965, at the beginning of the rebellion in the Dominican Republic, U.S. Ambassador W. Tapley Bennett declined a request by the opposing parties to mediate the rapidly growing dispute at a time when moderate leftists were still in control of the "constitutionalist" forces. Bennett's predecessor, John Bartlow Martin, states in his book *Overtaken by Events* that Bennett, having missed the chance at conciliation, probably had little choice but to bring in the Marines.

Martin fails to relate, however, a scene in which Bennett summoned a large portion of his staff and told them he was planning to call for help. After briefly describing the situation as he saw it, Bennett made clear that U.S. military forces, if summoned, would be ordered to thwart the attempted revolution, not just "protect U.S. lives and property." He then asked his staff if there were any alternative views or proposals. No one spoke.

• When John Bowling, a stimulating lecturer at the Foreign Service Institute, suggested that flag desecrators were philosophically identical to the bomb-throwing anarchists of previous decades, and that draft resisters were unmanly and cowardly, not one of the foreign service officers in his audience challenged the statement, despite Bowling's invitation to do so. No one spoke. After several moments of silence, Bowling himself felt compelled to express the other side.

Another illustration of how employees in the field are influenced by what their bosses want to hear comes from Patrick J. McGarvey, who used to work for the Defense Intelligence Agency. From 1964 through 1966, when U.S. generals wanted excuses for building up American troop strength in Vietnam, the DIA flooded Washington with reports of growing communist strength. Then, in 1967, the generals decided they wanted to show success. Washington was again flooded with cables, this time describing pacified villages and detailing enemy body counts. If your boss is a John Foster Dulles who does not like Sukarno or a Henry Kissinger who does not like Allende, you tend to find intelligence that says Sukarno and Allende are bad guys.

And if the boss wants his agency to expand, information that justifies expansion is what he'll get. When I worked for the Peace Corps in the early sixties, Sargent Shriver was eager to build the agency up as rapidly as possible. "Programmers" were sent overseas to solicit invitations for volunteers. Since many foreign officials were anxious to please the brother-in-law of the new American president, they were liberal in issuing invitations. And since each programmer was anxious to return to Washington "with a program in his pocket," as the saying went in those days, the invitations were not always subjected to careful scrutiny. The result was that hundreds of volunteers were dispatched to fictitious jobs or to places where they weren't really needed. The tendency to withhold from bosses what they don't want to hear is of course true of organizations generally. In the area of foreign affairs, however, its consequences can be catastrophic. It is doubtful, for example, that the Bay of Pigs fiasco would have occurred had someone had the courage to tell President Kennedy that with the cancellation of the air strike, which was to have wiped out Castro's air force, the invasion could not succeed. Warnings of Iraq's imminent invasion of Kuwait in the summer of 1990 also did not reach the highest level of authority. Two days before the invasion Pat Lang, a Defense Intelligence Agency employee, wrote a memo predicting that Saddam Hussein would move against Kuwait, but Lang received no reaction from his superiors. Then, the day before, he again warned that an invasion was coming "that night or the next morning." Colin Powell, head of the Joint Chiefs of Staff, wanted to advise the White House to issue a warning to Iraq, but he was overruled by Secretary of Defense Dick Cheney, who was convinced that Saddam was bluffing. At the State Department, the failure to warn was blamed on April Glaspie, the ambassador to Iraq, but she appears to have been motivated by the stake both she and the department had in the administration's policy of conciliating Saddam. The result of all this was that neither Defense nor State warned Bush in time at least in part because they wanted to think Bush's policy toward Iraq was working.

Joseph Burkholder Smith, a retired CIA official, has remarked that "policymakers will ignore intelligence that shows they have taken the wrong course of action, and the CIA station will oblige this inclination by providing intelligence that shows the policymakers they were right." Thus when South Vietnam was collapsing in March and April of 1975, Henry Kissinger and Gerald Ford didn't want to face what was happening, so Graham Martin, the U.S. ambassador, and Tom Polgar, the CIA station chief, kept feeding them overly optimistic reports. The result was that the United States failed to plan an orderly evacuation and left behind tens of thousands of Vietnamese who had been led to rely on American forces.

The man who told the truth about this episode was one of Polgar's subordinates, Frank Snepp, in a book called *Decent Interval*. The CIA sued Snepp. It promoted Polgar, leaving his colleagues a memorable lesson on how to get ahead.

Getting ahead is a factor in another characteristic of foreign service officers—their tendency to look inward and upward within the bureaucracy rather than outward, to the people of the country they are serving. Their survival network does not consist of campesinos sweating in Panamanian jungles or the starving poor of Calcutta; it is made up of other foreign service officers, who will sign their fitness reports and sit on their promotion boards, and of the Washington officials who can influence them.

Their primary concern is with Washington, where the promotion board and higher officials are. The drama of the day comes in reading cables from Washington and preparing cables to Washington—changing one word can trigger hours of debate—even though the preparer knows, as we have seen, that the chance of the cable's being read by the truly influential is less than one in ten. The only thing more important is Washington in the flesh, in the form of a high-ranking visitor. The embassy will then throb with vitality. The young aide sitting in one of the jump seats in the ambassador's limousine and listening to the ambassador exchange anecdotes with the visiting undersecretary waits expectantly for the moment when he can interject an incisive comment that will make him remembered as "that promising young officer in Dakar."

Second in importance to the Washington connection are relationships with the embassy itself. The process that John Kenneth Galbraith, who served as ambassador to India,

described as operating in the State Department also pre-
vails in embassies:

"When I went back [to the State Department] this time
one of my assistant secretary friends attended the Secretary's staff meeting from 9:15 until 10 A.M. Then he had
a meeting with the undersecretary on operations until
10:30. Then he took until 11:30 to inform his staff of what
went on at the earlier meeting. Whereupon they adjourned
to pass on the news to their staffs."

Day after day is spent in the make-believe of meetings
because there is so little else to do. Almost all of our embassies are overstaffed, as is the State Department itself.
Once we had an ambassador to Chile who reported directly
to the secretary of state. Then a Chile desk officer was
interposed in the hierarchy, followed by an assistant secretary for Latin America (with a deputy), then a regional
director for the west coast of Latin America (with his deputy), and finally an undersecretary for political affairs
(again, with a deputy). While technically the ambassador
now reports directly to the assistant secretary, there are at
least seven layers of titled officials between the secretary
and the ambassador that he has to worry about. And of
course each embassy has been stratified so that the ambassador presides over an elaborate chain of command, at the
bottom of which is the junior foreign service officer who
actually writes the first draft of the report.

All that's really needed is an ambassador or some other
official to write the report and a secretary of state to read
it. But the bureaucratic tendency to expand has generated
a stepladder of well-paid officials. If they did nothing at all,
that would be bad enough. But of course they have to add
something to every report to justify their titles, and in the
process reports and their encrustation of covering memoranda tend to become so ponderous and boring and devoid
of meaning that the secretary stops reading them, although
there are still a few diplomats around smart enough to

realize that only a concise cable has any real chance of being noticed at the top.

Third in importance in the life of the embassy is the relationship between the various elements of the American foreign service community. Interagency rivalries, such as those that have from time to time existed between the State Department and the CIA and between the Peace Corps and AID, consume tremendous amounts of time. Sometimes they may even have cost lives. For example, for years the foreign service insisted on distinguishing its officers from those of the CIA in the *Biographic Register*, a kind of studbook published by State. This was done in such a way that a hostile agent could easily identify the CIA people. The practice was stopped only after Richard Welch, a CIA station chief in Athens, was murdered in 1975. Fortunately, interagency rivalries are usually more benign. At one embassy meeting in Cameroon, the debate was about how to divide the shipment of Skippy peanut butter that had just arrived at the embassy PX.

The best example I know of the psychology of those who serve in U.S. missions overseas comes from this letter written to a friend of mine by an employee of AID in Saigon just six weeks before the city fell to the North Vietnamese (names have been changed)

"Shortly after my return we finally moved to USAIS II! Delays of a couple of months in the schedule, but made it up by mid-August. Much nicer quarters and location. I ended up with a nice little office, carpeted, etc. next to ADCCA with windows looking over the yard and entrance and shaded by the trees. . . . While I handled the overall coordination, when it came to space allocation, I just tried to see that each division received about the same amount of square footage on a per capita basis, and let each American Director decide how he would use it. Passing the buck nicely. I remember how much time and worry you had spent on that and so was looking for an easier way. Art Mason came out with an office the same size as mine (about 120 square feet), but located in the middle of CDI (cap. deve. and industry as it was named after you left). This made him very unhappy and he tried to get located on the floor close to ADCCA instead of the ground floor with the industry boys.

"When I returned I found the office in the midst of repairing IRRs on about nine capital projects for FY 75 presentation. . . . By the time that was completed, into preparing the documents for FY 76 program (now in place of IRR, two separate papers are needed to get the item in the Congressional Presentation). Without knowing what Congress would do to us in FY 75, we requested 14 projects totaling about $260 million! That exercise was completed by January 30. . . .

"The agency is going through a major RIF [reduction in force] which is being mishandled in every way possible. . . . The names finally came out Monday. Neil Anders and Eddie Jackson are the only two in CDI. Neil could retire and was expecting it; Eddie can't retire and his was unexpected by everybody. . . . Joe Falcone survived termination of his appointment by postponing actions for many months while filing about five grievances (several were valid, for the personnel people mishandled every aspect of his case), and is being transferred to Haiti as C.D. officer there. Ben Wyle is going to Abidjan. Jim Fisher is expecting and hoping to go to ROCAP (in Guatemala) for a tour that will set him up for retirement."

Remember, this letter was written in March 1975, as South Vietnam was falling apart. There is no mention of what was happening to the country in which the writer was working. Instead, while the South Vietnamese army was collapsing in the central highlands and the end of all of South Vietnam was only six weeks away, he writes only about budget, personnel, and the square footage, floor covering, and view from his office.

This is typical of the way far too many foreign service people think. Concerns internal to the mission are dominant. And of those, personnel policy is the most important. Here the AID employee is worried about reductions in staff, an uncommon event in government; more often the concern is about promotion. In the foreign service, for example, the shortage of significant work, combined with the reluctance of foreign service officers to quit, means that people must wait for what seems an eternity before they can move from the make-work jobs into any of the few with challenging duties.

John Kennedy's staff used to tell the president that if he had gone into the foreign service he would have been an FS-2 or FS-3 at the age he was elected, still ten years away from an ambassadorship. Richard Neustadt has said that fifteen years usually elapse between the time a foreign service officer is ready to assume responsibility and the time he gets it. Usually this waiting period starts between age thirty-five and forty and ends between age fifty and fifty-five.

Why do the officers stay? One motive is the government's retirement program, which so far has been more generous than most in the private sector. Another is the prestige of the foreign service, the reluctance to give up that institutional badge (which is the same reason so few Rhodes scholars come home early). In fact, as James Fallows has pointed out, the foreign service is a kind of lifelong Rhodes scholarship, a badge of status more important for the identity it gives the wearer than for what it requires him to accomplish. The badge confers, if not the touch of aristocracy it used to bring, at least a sense of class. The little secret no one lets out is that what one does after putting on the badge is not all that exciting.

Most young entrants say they are joining the service because they want to influence foreign policy. To show what happens later, John Harris quotes one official in his book *The Professional Diplomat*: "The trouble with most FSOs is that they are too concerned with *being* something or *becom-*

ing something—*being* a deputy chief of mission or *becoming* an ambassador—and not enough with *doing* anything."

A White House memorandum discussed the years foreign service officers spend waiting for responsibility: "[It] is a long wait. It is a period during which most officers will make at least a small blot on their copy books. The trauma of a bad (or mediocre) efficiency report is ordinarily enough to impress upon the recipient the value of caution and patience. Mid-career officers come to appreciate that the use of the word "abrasive" once in an FSO's files can be enough to counteract repeated appearances of words like 'creative' and 'resourceful' . . . so the art of becoming unabrasive becomes part of an FSO's stock in trade."

When William Macomber, a deputy undersecretary of state, testified before Congress, Senator Claiborne Pell asked him what an officer should do if he is asked to carry out a policy he thinks wrong. Macomber replied: "If he is the kind of person that has a pretty low boiling point on these matters, if he really feels untrue to himself to compromise in this way, then I think he is in the wrong business. Then I think he ought to be in politics, speaking out, or be a teacher or writer. Thus I think you have to accept certain inhibitions if you accept a career in the foreign service. On the other hand, there is a marvelous reward if you can stay in the foreign service and live with the kind of inhibition I described. Because then you are guaranteed a ringside seat in this terrific effort to make peace in the world."

Unfortunately, a ringside seat, watching rather than participating in crucial events, is all that most foreign service officers ever get. Usually they must settle for carrying the secretary's briefcase or looking over his shoulder during the great moments in diplomacy. But for the handful who finally do achieve Burns's dream and send that cable NEGOTIATIONS CONCLUDED, the satisfaction is immense.

Another reason foreign service officers used to like being

foreign service officers is that they became closely associated with the Harrimans and Lodges—with the elite group that has filled most of the cabinet and subcabinet jobs in the area of foreign affairs for most of our history. The members of this elite tended to have what William Colby calls "impeccable social and establishment credentials." They wrote for *Foreign Policy* and *Foreign Affairs*. They moved back and forth between government, law and investment firms, and the foundations. By the eighties, however, the elite had largely forgotten about public service as an obligation as it became ever more preoccupied with increasing its wealth and enjoying its pleasures.

Even so, an establishment tone continues to dominate the men and women of the foreign service. When such persons are in charge of foreign policy, there isn't likely to be any dramatic break with the past. Indeed, it is much more likely that past errors will be defended or protected from exposure.

The CIA has commonly used "national security" to justify nothing more than bureaucratic self-protection. For example, it tried to suppress part of a report written a week before Syria and Egypt invaded Israel in 1973 which stated that "the movement of Syrian troops and Egyptian military readiness are considered to be coincidental and not designed to lead to major hostilities."

As we noted earlier the intelligence agencies did only slightly better in foreseeing Iraq's invasion of Kuwait just two days before that unhappy event occurred. Even then, no one in the State Department saw the invasion as likely. In fact the ambassador, April Glaspie, thought the situation was stable enough to permit her to leave Iraq for a trip home, so she was not in Baghdad at the time of the invasion.

There have been plenty of similar errors. One of the most dramatic during the late seventies was the failure of the State Department and the CIA to anticipate the revolt against the shah in Iran. Here the significant factor may have been bureaucrats' tendency to rank personal pleasure above the public interest. Foreign service officers stayed in

Tehran, where they enjoyed a pleasant social life and, until the last moment, either did not hear of the discontent stirring in the provinces or did not realize the potential magnitude of the uprising.

Indeed, it might be said that the guiding principle of the foreign service—a tenet that is also followed religiously by most American journalists overseas—is Never Leave the City Where the Good Bars Are. That the CIA doesn't leave the cities either is suggested by the fact that all of its agents in Lebanon and Iran were in the respective capital cities, inside the U.S. embassies, when the one in Beirut was bombed and the one in Tehran was taken over by the mob. This principle has relieved the monotony of our lives by contributing greatly to the frequent occurrence of the unexpected in the Third World, from Jonestown to Vietnam.

Where you *can* find our foreign services are in places like London, where our embassy houses a staff of almost seven hundred people. Fifty-two of them work for the United States Information Agency. Their function is propaganda, promoting understanding of and sympathy for American policies, valiantly restraining the virulent anti-Americanism of the English people.

The State Department could learn something from the television networks. In 1990, ABC and NBC closed their Paris bureaus on the ground that Paris is no longer the news center it was. It may be that the State Department can't close down its embassy in the French capital, but certainly it could reduce the staff. London, Paris, and Rome staff patterns are based not on the importance of the posts to modern diplomacy—Moscow, Tokyo, and Peking are far more crucial—but on their desirability as places for diplomats to live and for Washington officials to visit.

But London, Paris, and Rome aren't the only overstaffed missions. In 1990 it was revealed that our embassy in Nicaragua had a support staff of 320 employees. Support staff means clerks, drivers, guards, and household servants. Why on earth should we need 320 in such a small country? In

Algeria the guards alone amount to 94 employees. If that shocks you, consider that in Thailand we employ 183 guards and in Egypt 204. Why do we need so many guards, especially since none of them are passed through security checks by the U.S. government? Nor, even when the Cold War was frigid, did we check the Soviet citizens we hired for support tasks at our embassy in Moscow. And "only the Soviets supplied by the UPKD, a state agency controlled by the KGB," writes Ronald Kessler in *Moscow Station*, "could work in foreign embassies in Moscow."

At last count we had 263 diplomatic missions abroad, including such posts as Nice, Seville, and Venice, which one had to suspect were chosen less because of their foreign policy significance than because of their attractiveness as assignments for foreign service officers.

If our foreign services waste their time on such frivolity, why have them? An official British study group has recommended abolishing Her Majesty's diplomatic service. We can't go that far—although it is tempting, isn't it?—because we do want the kind of foreign service officers and CIA agents who give us information we really need about other countries. But we could end either State Department or CIA representation in countries from which we do not need duplicate reports and abolish both in countries of little or no importance to us. (Why have a CIA station, as we do, in Ghana?) Where minimal facilities are needed to take care of lost tourists, we could make agreements with friendly countries so that, for example, we would represent Canada in Chad and Canada would represent us in Mauritania.

If even this seems too radical a departure, remember Ambassador Ellis Briggs's experience in Czechoslovakia, where he found his embassy performed more efficiently after most of the staff had been sent home. Bill Keller and Ann Cooper learned the same lesson when they went on from Morocco to visit the much smaller American diplomat community in Mali. A young AID economist who was serving in Mali but who had also worked in Morocco told them:

"Here I write a cable, and if it's correct and reasonable, it goes. It's just that people here have more things to do to occupy themselves than pick cables to pieces. In Rabat, everything was make-work."

In its issue of October 29, 1979, *Newsweek* reported that "six U.S. government officials abroad have been killed and 34 more involved in terrorist attacks or kidnappings so far this year." The very next week came the seizure of the hostages in Iran. Terrorism continued to take a fearful toll in the eighties, including the murder of the CIA station chief in Lebanon and of our ambassador to Pakistan. Should we ask people to risk their lives for the sake of make-work?

There is some reason to hope that terrorism is waning. The State Department reported that international terrorist incidents declined from a high of 856 in 1988 to 455 in 1990. But even the latter figure must be troubling to our diplomats.

Even more troubling is the fact that, since John Kennedy became president in 1961, control of diplomacy has been passing from the hands of State Department officials to those of the White House National Security Council staff. From the time Kennedy named McGeorge Bundy director of the NSC the White House has been seizing control of diplomacy from the diplomats. In the eighties, the potential for evil in this arrangement became manifest as a set of irresponsible incompetents brought us disaster in Lebanon—recall the bombing of the marine barracks in Beirut, for which Robert McFarlane was largely responsible—and the Iran-contra scandal, which was orchestrated by McFarlane, John Poindexter, and Oliver North, all members of Reagan's NSC staff.

The State Department had more power under George Bush because the president's friend James Baker was secretary. But crucial policy decisions still tended to be made by the NSC or, when the NSC was not interested in the subject or when the secretary chose to assert his influence with the president, by Baker and a handful of his top cronies in Foggy Bottom—Margaret Tutwiler, Robert Zoellick, and Dennis Ross. The professional diplomats were ignored. The surest sign the Bush-Baker group did not take Iraq's threat to Kuwait seriously was that they allowed the final, crucial meeting with Saddam Hussein to be conducted by a career foreign service ambassador, April Glaspie.

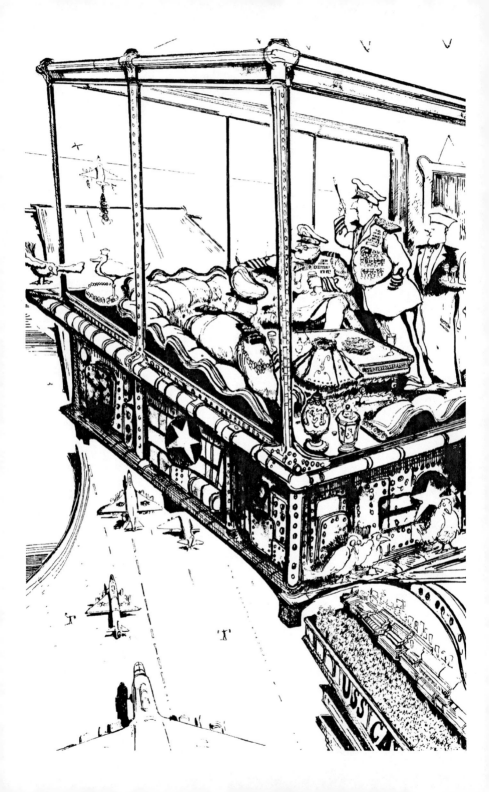

5.

THE MILITARY

Although there was marked improvement in the overall performance of the military between Vietnam and the Gulf War—even between Grenada and the Gulf—many problems persist. One is the contrast between the way officers and enlisted personnel are treated. It is true that the compensation of enlisted men and women was increased substantially during the seventies and eighties, but grating differences remain between the way enlistees and their officers live. Visit almost any military base and see how much better officers' housing is compared to the enlisted men's. And compare the often luxurious officers' clubs to the relatively simple social facilities of the enlisted men. When things go wrong, the officers usually do the investigating and the enlisted men usually take the blame. Of the first 126 soldiers relieved from duty in an army recruiting scandal, only three were officers. And when things go really wrong, it's the enlisted men who pay. When the battleship *Iowa*'s gun turret blew up, 46 enlisted men were killed. Only one officer died.

The differences in the way officers and enlisted men live

are illustrated by this passage from Stuart Loory's book *Defeated: Inside America's Military Machine*:

"Rear Admiral James E. Ferris commanded an aircraft carrier task force . . . in the South China Sea. . . . Ferris's quarters, known as "admiral's country" aboard ship, were . . . like a New York Central Park South luxury apartment. . . .

"A huge green plant grew against one wall. . . . The planter rested on thick beige carpeting that helped deaden the bone-shaking noise of aircraft launching and recovery operations. There was not a stray bit of dust on the glass-topped coffee table nor an ash in any of the heavy glass ashtrays. The thought was inescapable that orderlies were ever present, waiting for the tiniest bit of refuse to accumulate, sweeping it up as soon as the admiral left the room. On one wall, a walnut credenza held a stereo tape player. The admiral's desk was set against the opposite wall.

"The sofa was covered in a nubby white fabric. It was functional but soft, enveloping a visitor in instant comfort and security. Just outside the doorway to the study, a marine aide stood attentively, if not always at attention, waiting to carry out the admiral's every wish. In the small galley, two Filipino messmen were preparing a chicken dinner for the evening.

"The admiral's dining room . . . could seat ten comfortably around an oval table covered with starched white linen. The silverware was heavy and glistening. The meals were served with painstaking etiquette by white-coated attendants. . . .

"Belowdecks, the crew was jammed together, 150 men to each open, windowless, poorly lighted, ill-ventilated bay. They lived one atop the other, three bunks high, with no privacy and little storage space, with the constant noise of the ship's operations jarring them. They took their meals in windowless, low-ceilinged mess spaces that doubled as warehouses for the bombs and rockets the airplanes would use."

All the resentments that such experiences produced were exacerbated by the contrast between the enlisted man's twelve months on the firing line in Vietnam and the five- or six-month combat tours of officers. Platoon leaders and company commanders were "rotated" in and out of units before they had a chance to get to know their men or to master their jobs. The Gulf War was so short that rotation did not become a problem, but if it had lasted for more than six months, rotation would have been inevitable.

One reason for these rotations is that there are far too many officers in the military. As of 1990, there were 32,000 lieutenant colonels and commanders in the army, air force, marines, and navy, compared to 36,000 at the height of World War II—when there were six times as many enlisted men. There were 14 generals for each division in 1945. In 1990 the figure was 22, the same as during Vietnam. Yet only three American generals were killed by enemy fire in Vietnam. None died in the Gulf War. By contrast, 223 German generals—a third of the total number—were killed during World War II; in fact, the casualty rate among German generals was higher than among enlisted men. This sharing of risk helps explain the bond between German officers and enlisted men that created the second most efficient army in modern history. The most efficient military machine of the era, Israel's, is one-tenth the size of the U.S. military but has only one twenty-fifth the number of major generals. Israel's air force has only one major general; ours has 120.

The Vietnam War, because of its unpopularity, and because the educated elite got draft deferments, also had an unfortunate effect on the social composition of the military. The proportion of college graduates in the services dropped 75 percent between World War II and Vietnam. Now enlisted men come from poor and lower middle-class backgrounds and officers from the lower to middle range of the middle class. The result is a military that does not represent the variety of talents and points of view of the country as a whole, a military that has almost no connection with a significant part of the population—the very part, in fact, that tends to produce the leaders of the rest of our institutions.

One evil consequence of this change became dramatic during Vietnam: Members of the lower classes, scorned by their betters, who had the resouces to avoid the draft, did almost all of the dying. And when a terrorist bomb destroyed the marine barracks in Beiruit in 1983, it was again lower-class enlisted men who did the dying.

Maury Maverick managed to pry out of the Pentagon the religious affiliations of the 220 who died that day in Beirut. Of the 220, more than half were Catholic or Baptists. Upper-class faiths were radically underrepresented—there were no Unitarians, Quakers, or Jews, and only two Presbyterians and two Episcopalians. In the Gulf War, the dead included three Episcopalians, one Unitarian, and no Jews.

Just stop and think: How many rich people do you know in the military? How many graduates of Harvard and Yale? If you happen to be among the more affluent yourself, ask yourself if you have any relatives in the military. When *Time* magazine recently asked whites and blacks if they had family members serving in the Middle East, the percentage of blacks who replied yes was more than twice that of the whites. Still, the percentage of whites with relatives in the military was four times that of congressmen—even when the representatives' in-laws were counted.

Another side effect of this uneven social composition is the general ignorance of the educated elite about military affairs, because its members have not served in the military or even had friends who have done so. Thus when the question arises as to what kinds of planes, tanks, and missiles the country needs or what the role of the army or the air force should be, intellectuals tend to adopt, through lack of real knowledge, clichéd positions that are usually stupidly antimilitary but are sometimes equally stupidly pro. Just recall for a moment the embarrassingly ignorant questions asked by members of the press, almost all of whom are from the educated elite, during the Gulf War briefings.

A further reason for those five- or six-month tours for officers in Vietnam is that the officers were getting their "tickets punched," a phrase that aptly describes what an officer has to do to get ahead in the military. The most essential ticket punch of all is combat command. There was tremendous competition for troop commands in Vietnam, from platoon to company to battalion to regiment to division. To give more officers a chance to serve in combat jobs, tours were limited to a few months each.

Although ticket punching didn't become a factor in the Gulf War because of its brevity, there are other ways of getting one's ticket punched that continue to be crucial to an officer's success. For example, the officers most likely to get ahead in the military went to West Point or Annapolis or the Air Force Academy. As of 1991 West Point graduates constituted twice the percentage of generals as they did of other army officers; Annapolis graduates constituted three times the comparable percentage of admirals over other navy officers.

Here are other methods of getting your ticket punched in the army (there are comparable strategies in the air force and navy):

• Attend the Command and General Staff College at Fort Leavenworth, Kansas. This is the most prestigious of all the army's staff colleges. You are selected for it by a special board when you are a captain or a major. Class rank is even more important here than at West Point because you're studying bread-and-butter issues in military strategy and tactics and your record will follow you throughout your career.

• Work at the Pentagon, preferably in the office of the secretary of defense. There you will have the opportunity to meet powerful figures from the Defense Department and other parts of the executive branch as well as from Congress. This is where you attract the patrons and sponsors who will make sure that you get the choice assignments. A tour at the White House's National Security Council serves the same purpose. Alexander Haig and Colin Powell worked at both the OSD and the NSC.

• Get a graduate degree at a civilian university. This "requirement" came into existence during the days of Robert McNamara in the Kennedy and Johnson administrations, when being an intellectual whiz kid was the thing. Almost all generals have one or more such degrees today.

• It is essential that you attend Defense Information School at Fort Benjamin Harrison, Indiana, or acquire some other kind of public relations experience that will teach you how to handle the press. The top people in the Gulf War— Norman Schwarzkopf, Colin Powell, Lieutenant General Thomas Kelly—each had obviously become highly skilled in this art.

• Attend the National Defense University. Located on the grounds of Fort Leslie McNair in southwest Washington, D.C., this school attracts high-level civilian officials as well as lieutenant colonels from the army and air force and commanders from the navy. The curriculum focuses not on military tactics but rather on larger political and economic issues that will prepare you for high-level participation in global strategy and national security policy.

John Fialka tells the story of how one general built his network:

"General Bernard W. Rogers . . . graduated from West Point in 1943, . . . started out as a platoon leader in the 70th Infantry Division. . . . General Maxwell D. Taylor, . . . looking around for a young officer to assist him as commandant of West Point, . . . asked who . . . the brightest and most promising officer [was], and 'four people told me Bernie Rogers,' recalls Taylor. In 1947 Rogers was awarded a Rhodes scholarship and went to Oxford University in England, where for three years he studied philosophy, politics, and economics. . . . He saw his first combat in Korea in

1952, when he won a silver star as the commander of a 2nd Infantry Division battalion. From the late 1950s through the mid-1960s, Rogers held a number of key staff positions in the Pentagon, culminating in 1963 when he was appointed executive officer to Taylor, then chairman of the joint chiefs.

"From November 1966 to August 1967, he [was an] assistant division commander of the 1st Infantry Division in Vietnam. After that . . . commandant of West Point. In 1971 Rogers helped insure his ascendancy. He became chief of legislative liaison in the office of the secretary of the army and gained the respect of a number of powers on the House and Senate Armed Services committees." All those ticket punches ultimately got Rogers appointed to a plum assignment as supreme commander of NATO.

There are both good and bad aspects to the present system of ticket punching. It's good for officers to know that command of combat troops is important to their careers because as they rise in responsibility their decisions will reflect firsthand knowledge of what life is like for combat units. And because they have been exposed to this true performance test they are more likely to be skilled than the average civil servant of comparable rank, who can escape such tests throughout his career. But it is not good for this experience to be sought, as it was in Vietnam, at the cost of those attenuated tours that were so destructive to the morale of the troops. Nor is it pleasant that the system makes young military officers pray for a war in order to get ahead.

And, as we have already seen with the foreign service, the frequent change of assignment required by the ticket-punching system produces low institutional memory and repeated discoveries of the wheel at each post. There is an accompanying lack of interest in long-range improvement of any unit. The officer cares about how it looks today so that he will look good, but not about how it will look tomorrow, because he won't be there tomorrow. And because he won't be there tomorrow he does not develop the loyalty to and pride in his unit that throughout history produced outstanding battalions and regiments.

A farcical aspect of the system is the Officer Efficiency Reports (OERs), a series of performance ratings each officer gets every six months as he progresses from second lieutenant to major general. The OERs, like the dollar, academic grades, and annual merit ratings that produce raises for almost all civil servants, are badly inflated. "Commanding officers know," Nicholas Lemann has written, "that good scores make for happy subordinates and that bad scores, rather than serving notice of temporary failing, can wreck careers. So the maximum score of 200 is common and a 185 is a disaster. If you average below 195, it's thought impossible to make major.

"To be sure, there are subtle ways a rater can damn an officer without having to give him a low rating. For instance, a rater can say in his typed comments on the officer that he did a "superior job" and leave [the officer's] career in ruins. Elsewhere on the report "superior" appears as the second-best adjective in a hierarchy of praise that's led by "outstanding"; so to call an officer superior is to call him second-rate. Also, promotion boards go through OERs so fast that any reservation-expressing word like "but" or "despite" or "although" is thought to stand out as a red flag of disapproval regardless of its context.

"Because no officer who wants to advance himself can afford a bad report, no officer can afford to cross his boss."

The tendency of bureaucrats to take a dim view of whistle-blowers is particularly marked in the military. Lieutenant General William R. Peers's investigation of the My Lai massacre is a case in point. From the moment top officials at the Pentagon instituted the body count as the measure of success in Vietnam, commanders began to pressure their subordinates to produce bodies. And because the subordinates wanted to please their superiors, they began to produce a lot of bodies, which meant shooting a lot of people, including civilians. At My Lai, somewhere between 175 and 400 Vietnamese noncombatants were slaughtered by soldiers of the American division under the leadership of General Bernard Kosters, who, along with his key subordinates, immediately instituted a cover-up that took investigators under Peers several years to expose. Peers's final report identified thirty officers who were involved in the cover-up. Of these, only four were actually put on trial by the army, and three were acquitted by military judges. Peers, for his part, was rewarded by having his career, which had been on the full-general track, completely derailed. He retired, still a lieutenant general, in 1972.

Other examples of how the armed forces deal with those who reveal military scandals abound. When Ernest Fitzgerald, a civilian employee of the air force, told Congress the truth about the C-5A in 1968, the air force fired him. After Fitzgerald won back his job through a court fight, the generals made sure he was given nothing to do. Fast forward to 1986, when the army rewarded Colonel James Burton, who had revealed critical defects in the Bradley fighting vehicle, with exile from the Pentagon to a meaningless job in Dayton, Ohio. The signal given by the treatment of Peers, Fitzgerald, and Burton is that you'd better keep your mouth shut if you want to stay out of trouble.

Besides the less-than-above-board actions taken by defense officials in their bureaucratic struggle to survive, the moral rot from Vietnam also spread to the army as a whole. Even West Point, with its hallowed traditions of honor, did not escape. The early seventies witnessed the worst cheating scandal in the history of the cadet corps, implicating hundreds instead of just the handful of cadets who had been involved in such episodes in the past.

The army said it was concerned, leading Lieutenant General Andrew J. Goodpaster, superintendent at West Point, to include morals and ethics in the academy's curriculum. "Under the new program," reported Drew Middleton in the *New York Times* in August 1978, "plebes or first-year students must take two ethics courses. One course will be required in each subsequent year." Goodpaster explained to Middleton that the new courses would teach the young officer how to act when his superior presses him for such things as fake body counts. "All he has to do," Goodpaster said, "is to ask his senior officer, 'Sir, are you asking me to send in a fake report?' That will do it."

If you find that dialogue a little hard to believe, you may be fortified in your skepticism by the revelation by Herman Smith, former coach of the army's football team, in December 1978 that Goodpaster himself had participated in the cover-up of scandals about the recruiting of athletes for academy teams. And things don't seem to have improved. In 1990, Professor Ralph P. Santoro, who had taught at the Naval Academy for twenty-five years and rose to the chairmanship of the electrical engineering department, was dismissed for refusing to raise students' grades. He was, in other words, fired for refusing to lie about what he thought were proper marks. So what's the real message about honor?

The aspect of moral blindness in the military that probably costs taxpayers the most is the increasingly frequent custom of allowing thousands of officers to leave the service each year to work for private companies that have contracts with the armed forces. Not only do we pay them two salaries—their retirement pensions and their salaries from the contractors, which are usually financed by the U.S. Treasury—but they are tempted during their service careers to soft-pedal any criticism they might have of the contractors who, as potential employers, are an important part of their survival network. Consequently, contractors are more likely to get away with building defective planes or tanks or ships, or what is more common, with charging too much for them.

The best way to end this type of corruption in the Pentagon is to forbid military retirees from working for military contractors. As things stand now, far too many Pentagon officers spend half their day thinking of how to position themselves for a good job with McDonnell Douglas or General Dynamics when they leave the service. This means that they lean over backward to be tender to defense contractors when it is their duty to lean over backward to be tough.

Another aspect of the system that is unduly hard on taxpayers is that it permits retirement after only twenty years' service. The original reason for early retirement was that most military jobs in days gone by were physically arduous. If you had to spend twenty years charging over hills on foot—or even on horseback—you needed the promise of early retirement to help you endure. But now things have changed. Most military jobs are essentially desk-bound and technical, clerical, or managerial in nature. The General Accounting Office found that 93 percent of retiring enlisted personnel who were taking pensions after an average of twenty-one years of service had been working in support-type jobs that had none of the hardships of combat. So an early retirement designed to reward combat-weary troops is being used instead to benefit paperwork-weary bureaucrats.

The pension system is just part of a larger pattern of our fiscal indulgence of the military. For example, taxpayers subsidize commissaries where service families buy food and other items at a 25 percent discount—this while officers receive more in overall compensation and benefits than do federal civilian employees in comparable grades of the civil service.

All this overindulgence creates a psychology among military personnel that leads them to think they have a right to take us to the cleaners. The *Washington Post* took a look at the taxpaying habits of members of the military living in the Washington, D.C., area, and found that 51.9 percent did not file local tax returns in the District of Columbia— or anywhere else. They may live in Washington, but they raise the make-believe principle to new heights by claiming "residence" in one of the states that exempts military personnel from taxation. Thus the taxpayers who pay their salaries have to pay their taxes as well.

If you can't make up your mind whether to laugh or cry, cry. But at the same time realize that most members of the military are not at heart as selfish as they appear to be. Change the institutional imperatives that govern their lives and they will change.

There are four simple steps to take: (1) provide that no one can become an officer without beginning at the bottom of the enlisted ranks and working his way up—earning promotions and assignments to places like the service academies and the defense colleges—solely on the basis of demonstrated competence; (2) restore candor to the process of evaluating both officers and enlisted men; (3) require at least thirty years' service before retirement; (4) draft the rich. The last is the most essential step of all. How can members of the upper classes expect the soldier or sailor to be a dedicated, unselfish patriot when they refuse to share his risk? Why should he die for people who look down on him, who secretly think he is a sucker?

6.

COURTS AND REGULATORS

In 1971, a jury in New York City was split eleven to one in favor of a robbery conviction, but the case was dismissed by the judge after only twelve hours of deliberation because he had another engagement. This enabled the robber to escape punishment because a second trial would have violated his constitutional rights. What was the other engagement? A trip to Europe.

I can imagine many of my readers saying, "That New York case was in 1971. Maybe the judge didn't consider his duties to be pressing, but haven't things changed since then? Aren't the courts now overworked?"

The answer is that a few big city criminal courts did become clogged with drug cases in the seventies and eighties. And in civil courts around the country there was a substantial increase in the number of suits filed. But on the whole, most judges manage to continue to lead a soft life by minimizing the number of cases that are actually tried or heard on appeal.

On May 9, 1989, the *Manhattan Lawyer* sent reporters

into all forty-five full-time courtrooms of the New York State Supreme Court felony division. They found that the average court was in session only four hours and twenty-seven minutes a day. Sixty-two percent spent less than five hours in session; 42 percent started work after 10:00 A.M. None was in session more than six hours and thirty-five minutes.

In Massachusetts, judges get six weeks' vacation a year in addition to sick leave, a week off for "personal" time, and three weeks' "educational" leave. Still they claim they are overworked. So in 1990 the *Boston Globe* looked into when these judges actually left the courthouse. Six judges were photographed making their exits. The exact times of departure were 3:33 P.M., 3:20 P.M., 2:35 P.M., 12:05 P.M., 12:01 P.M., and 11:10 A.M. One judge was described by the *Globe* as "leaving a courtroom so silent and empty that his court officer was able to lie down on a bench and nap the afternoon away."

Perhaps, you say, the judges were rushing home to write opinions in the privacy of their dens. Not very likely, since most of the judges covered in the *Globe* and *Manhattan Lawyer* stories were below the level where opinion writing is the main part of the job. Where opinion writing is central to the job, at the appellate level, we see the same relaxed approach that the *Manhattan Lawyer* and the *Boston Globe* found in the lower courts. In 1989 the *Recorder,* a San Francisco legal newspaper, conducted a study of how long on average it took judges of the Ninth Circuit of the U.S. Court of Appeals to produce an opinion. The four hardest-working jurists took under 100 days. But the average for all the judges was 147 days. Seven took more than 200, one 307.

The typical judge loves the rewards of office and tends to be imperious in asserting and defending them. Thus Richard Neely, a West Virginia Supreme Court justice, fired his secretary because she refused to baby-sit for his children. When Warren Burger, the chief justice of the United States from 1973 to 1986, was accused of having a government car pick up his daughter's laundry, he indignantly replied, "It was *my* laundry!"

The first thing to understand about our system of justice is that it is designed to serve the convenience of the people who staff it. If you have ever been a juror or a witness, you probably wasted days, even weeks, waiting to be called while the judge, lawyers, and clerks conferred on matters that might have ranged from solemn to obscene. Whatever the purpose of these discussions, it is seldom to make the system suit the needs of the witnesses or jurors—or, for that matter, of plaintiffs or defendants, although on occasion, as in the case of the defendant in that New York robbery case, one of the parties might be an unintentional beneficiary.

The cruelest result of this system is perhaps the plea bargain, especially when a penniless criminal defendant is assigned a court-appointed lawyer who receives a fixed fee or salary regardless of how much time he spends on the case. The lawyer's self-interest is served by minimizing the time and effort he devotes to his client's cause, and he is therefore tempted to persuade the client to plead guilty even though he may have a good defense. And the defense attorney has a good chance of getting the prosecution to accept a reduced charge, even if the prosecution is certain of the defendant's guilt. Again the reason is that the prosecutor, a salaried employee, is paid the same whether he tries the case or not. Trying a case is a lot of work. Not trying a case is *not* a lot of work. And if the docket is clogged, say with more drug cases that the most diligent prosecutor could possibly try, the temptation to plea-bargain becomes compelling. Most criminal cases are therefore settled without trial by the process of plea bargaining between the prosecutor and the defense attorney. Sometimes the innocent are convicted, but more often the guilty get off too easily—all because lawyers don't want to work. Judges almost always approve plea bargains because they too are paid their salaries regardless of whether cases are tried, and they too want to get an early start on that fishing trip. The fishing trips, and the ability to set their own schedule, may have something to do with why judgeships—particularly federal judgeships, which are well-paid lifetime jobs—are looked upon as rewards. And when people look upon jobs as rewards rather than opportunities to work, there is a problem.

A lot of judges see their jobs as rewards either for distinguished careers as practicing lawyers or professors or, conspicuously since 1981, for devoted adherence to conservative doctrines. In states that have Republican senators, a federal district court judgeship is often a reward for political support in a senatorial campaign. As a general rule, presidents have appointed federal district judges only on nomination or at least endorsement by a senator of their party from the state where the court is located. Jimmy Carter made a brief effort to change this practice when he became president, but he was by and large unsuccessful.

Donald Dale Jackson, in his book *Judges,* quotes J. Sam Perry of Illinois on how he got his federal judgeship:

"I gambled," he said. "I saw a man—Paul Douglas—who looked as though he might be elected to the Senate. I backed him, and as a result I had his support. . . . I tried to obtain the appointment once before and learned that it requires not one but two senators. . . . I was out of politics and they did not need me. I decided I had better get back into politics, which I did. I learned that everyone shoots at the number one choice, so I told each of the senators not to make me first. . . . That proved to be pretty good strategy—everybody else was shot off, and, no use lying about it, I helped to shoot them off. The result was I landed on top."

Generous campaign contributions also help. Even children can contribute, as in the case of Gilbert Merritt, a nominee for a judgeship on the Circuit Court of Appeals sponsored by Senator Jim Sasser of Tennessee. In response to a question by the Senate Judiciary Committee about the $1,000 contributions made by each of his three children, ages ten, eleven, and twelve, to Senator Sasser's campaign,

Merritt said the contributions were the children's own idea: "The children were well aware of the need for campaign contributions and were very well aware at that time of the need for such contributions by Senator Sasser."

This is not to say that such political appointees are without merit. On the contrary, most of them are quite able. (Their problem, remember, is the "reward" psychology that goes with the job.) The person who manages a senator's campaign is often a successful trial attorney with experience that is highly relevant to a district judgeship. In fact, political appointees may be more qualified for district judgeships than the "merit" nominees of the bar association panels. The latter are usually from the big law firms, where the training is less in courtroom skills than in the brief- and memo-writing skills that are more suitable for the higher federal courts—the Circuit Court of Appeals and the Supreme Court.

The men and women who become judges on these appellate courts are often chosen because they are supported by a powerful group, as Thurgood Marshall was backed by the NAACP, or because they enjoy wide respect within their profession, as did Lewis Powell, a former president of the American Bar Association. During the Reagan and Bush administrations, fidelity to conservative principles has been perhaps even more important in appellate court nominations than we have noted it is at the district court level.

Over the years, however, it is the Powells who have dominated the appellate bench. Sometimes they come from the faculties of the great law schools (Felix Frankfurter, for example, was at Harvard), but more often they have spent most of their lives working for major law firms in our larger cities. Many of them, whether they have come from faculty or firm, were "on the law review"—that is, they were staff members for their law schools' publications, which analyze recent decisions and trends in the law—jobs usually reserved for the best of the second- and third-year students.

These top students often go on to become law clerks for

appellate judges. A great many of these judges were once clerks themselves—the present chief justice, William Rehnquist, clerked for Justice Robert Jackson in 1952—which helps explain the high opinion justices have of their clerks and their heavy reliance on them. Whatever the reason, these law clerks (distinguish them from the administrative clerks who serve as traffic managers and recorders of the court's business) have extraordinary power in the nation's legal system. In fact, they are the best examples I know of something I call "subordinate power," which is a powerful force in the life of most organizations. The person in charge wants to be liked and respected by the people who work for him. Therefore just as the employee tries to please the boss, the boss will try to please the employee.

I can think of many times I have been saved from folly by employees who talked me into a more sensible course. I can also think of times when I've made mistakes because of a desire to please the people who worked with me. When I was working in the government, the director of my agency doubled my modest bureaucratic empire by adding a new division. I was eager to win the respect and affection of its employees, so I immediately endorsed their budget request for $1 million and worked hard to get it approved. Congress gave us $500,000, but it turned out that we were able to spend only $385,000 even after using every end-of-the-fiscal-year spending technique known to the bureaucratic world.

So subordinate power can be harmful. You see its worst effects in the new cabinet secretary who brings to the job a determination to reform the department but who quickly becomes the prisoner of his minions. The most powerful subordinates in America may be the clerks who serve the justices of the Supreme Court. They advise the justices and draft opinions for them. Sometimes they even write the opinions, as this anecdote about Thurgood Marshall from Bob Woodward and Scott Armstrong's *The Brethren* reveals:

"A clerk once pointed out, 'You said that the right to privacy must go further than the home.'

'No,' Marshall retorted, he had never said that.

'Yes,' the clerk insisted.

'No, never,' Marshall was sure. 'Show me.'

The clerk brought the bound opinions.

Marshall read the relevant section.

'That's not my opinion. That's the opinion of a clerk from the prior term.'"

The clerks also screen appeals. Consider the importance of just that function. In the thirties, the Supreme Court received about 1,000 cases a year and gave hearings and wrote opinions on about 150 of them. In 1990–91, the number of opinions was about the same but the number of appeals had risen to more than 4,000, and the role of the clerks in choosing which would be heard had grown proportionally. This means that, instead of each justice having one or two clerks, two of the justices now have three and seven have four. Notice that it was not the justices but the clerks who absorbed the increased workload.

The greater number of cases appealed before the Supreme Court is but one manifestation of the law's unique potential for growth. Every time a lawyer files a suit he creates business not only for himself but for the lawyer or lawyers who will have to represent the other side. Americans have not been blind to this kind of opportunity: Between 1963 and 1991, the number of law students more than doubled, to 132,433. The number of lawyers in New York City alone rose from 49,386 to 77,890 in just the decade of the eighties. Determining motivation in any human endeavor is a murky matter, but two motives stand out: making money and making law.

The July/August 1991 issue of the *American Lawyer* revealed that fifty-seven U.S. law firms had revenues in excess of $100 million in the preceding year. In 1989, *Forbes* magazine reported that the top ten trial lawyers in the United

States each earned more than $5 million in the preceding year. If you think "Deep Pocket" refers to some Watergate-type scandal, you're wrong. It's lawyer slang to describe a client, usually a corporation, with an apparently limitless capacity to pay fees. When a lawyer has hooked one of these dream clients he can, as another elegant lawyerly phrase puts it, "keep the meter running."

The kind of case lawyers love is exemplified by the one that arose out of the collapse of the Franklin National Bank. The lawyers for Michele Sindona, an Italian financier whose role in the bank's failure was such that he has strenuously resisted extradition, managed to con the presiding judge into disqualifying himself for having made a harmless joke about Sindona. The result was that the other clients in the case, who had already spent $1 million in legal fees, had to start all over again, while Mr. Sindona and all the lawyers laughed and laughed.

Perhaps an antitrust case tried in 1979 came closest to revealing the relative rank of money and justice in the eyes of members of the legal profession. The plaintiff's lawyers gave the court a twenty-one-page memorandum on behalf of their clients' case, but to support their petition for $1.1 million in fees, they produced two hundred neatly bound and carefully indexed pages.

By 1991, more than a third of a $1.5 billion fund set up to compensate victims of asbestos-related diseases had gone to lawyers. A Minneapolis firm charged $208,733 for winning $3,000 in damages. In Louisiana a federal judge caught a lawyer billing for more than twenty-four hours a day, not just once and perhaps inadvertently, but an unmistakably larcenous six times. In Illinois, Judge Frank Easterbrook found another attorney billing half his time to a case in which the appeal was pending—a period during which only the appellate court, not the lawyer, has any work to do. And in 1990 a federal appeals court found that more than half of the 6,652 hours billed in a Texas case were for "revision," "conferences," and "monitoring."

Aaron Epstein, in an article for the Knight-Ridder news service in 1991, found that two major causes of inflated fees were overstaffing and unnecessary work. I personally witnessed the effects of both a few years ago, when a congressman who felt that *The Washington Monthly* had been a bit too severe in its comments about him engaged a Washington law firm to act on his behalf. One of the firm's partners called me and arranged an appointment. When he arrived at my office he had two other lawyers in tow. We proceeded to state our respective positions, which took about fifteen minutes. Another fifteen minutes made clear that there was nothing to be gained by further discussion. I had other work to do and was hoping they would leave. But they just sat there, going over the same ground again and again for another half hour. Finally they departed. I escorted them to the street, where a limousine was waiting to take them back to their office.

I thought for a moment about the fees that would be charged for the limousine for the hour it had waited, and for the half hour it took to make the round trip to and from the office, and for the one and a half hours each of the three lawyers had devoted to the visit, not to mention the time spent conferring with each other and the client before and after the visit. I figured that the client already owed several thousand dollars for a matter that could have been handled just as easily by a few phone conversations.

I am convinced that these practices and the conscious or unconscious cynicism they reflect are not just a problem among a few shady shysters but are commonplace among the most respected law firms in the nation. The firm involved in the case I just described, for example, was not some fly-by-night outfit, but Clifford & Warnke, then one of Washington's most eminent legal partnerships.

Some lawyers want more than money. Take the late Abe Fortas, who made hundreds of thousands of dollars a year as a partner in another of Washington's leading firms, Arnold, Fortas & Porter. Before he and his partners formed their firm, they had "made law" in the thirties. Working for the very modest federal salaries of the time, they actually wrote much of the legislation of the New Deal. Even after he went into private practice, Fortas occasionally took cases he thought were important even though his compensation for them was slight or nonexistent. In one, the case of *Gideon* v. *Wainwright,* he in effect made legislation by persuading the Supreme Court to rule that the Constitution requires defendants accused of felonies to be represented by a lawyer. The money motive proved Fortas's undoing, however. Soon after he was nominated by Lyndon Johnson to be chief justice of the Supreme Court, it was revealed that he had continued to serve as a paid legal adviser to Louis Wolfson, a defendant in cases that could have gone to the Supreme Court, where Fortas would have ruled on them.

But if Fortas's desire to make money got him into trouble, it was his desire to make law that got our legal system into trouble—both the regulatory law that he and his partners had pioneered in the thirties and the criminal law that was the outgrowth of his victory in the *Gideon* case.

Let's look at the latter first. Immortalized by Anthony Lewis of the *New York Times* in a book called *Gideon's Trumpet,* the *Gideon* case had every young lawyer eager to make a name filing writ after writ to free criminal defendants by making new law. Some of the new law, like the *Gideon* case, represented clearly desirable reform. But the overall effect was to help the guilty escape punishment. If you've ever practiced criminal law, you know the police occasionally arrest the innocent but usually get only the obviously guilty. Yet fewer than 25 percent of the people arrested on felony charges in New York City are convicted—104,000 convicted out of 473,000 arrests. (These figures, which cover the period 1989–90, were obtained from police and district attorneys' offices.)

What do these statistics mean in human terms? Here is the story of the shooting of a woman named Sally Ann Morris as described by the *Washington Post*:

"She and her boyfriend, Henry Miller, were walking down 33rd Street, heading for an M Street restaurant . . . when two men approached. As they passed the couple, one of the men pulled out a gun, cocked it and stuck it in Sally Morris's back.

"Instinctively, Miller grabbed her and they started to run. . . . She heard gunfire and felt a slap at her back. . . . The bullet ripped through her intestinal tract and lodged in her lower abdomen. . . . Doctors had to perform a colostomy, rerouting the undamaged intestinal tract to a substitute opening in her lower abdomen. This type of operation allows body waste to be passed into a disposable plastic bag attached to the new opening.

"Compounding all this is the fear that the ordeal is not yet over and that her assailants may return to kill her. Four suspects arrested in the case, who were released on personal recognizance, pending trial, promptly disappeared and are at large today."

The Bail Reform Act of 1965, passed in the first flush of *Gideon,* applied to all federal jurisdictions, including the District of Columbia. It provided, among other things, that "no financial condition shall be imposed to assure the safety of any other person or the country." In other words, bail could not be required to protect Sally Morris or the people of Washington from the man who had shot her.

What can we do, then, for the victims of crime? The court's answer in the case of Sally Morris was "witness protection": She could be locked up for her own protection while the criminals who shot her went free until the trial. That makes sense, doesn't it? Sally Morris in jail, the criminals on the street?

The logic was so outrageous that Congress had to act. The Bail Reform Act of 1984 provided that the safety of the community could be considered in determining whether a suspect should get bail. The Supreme Court upheld the new provision in 1987. But many judges continue to be influenced by the Morris case's legacy of solicitude for the accused which explains why we still read of murders that are committed by criminals let out on bail even though they have violent records.

Generally, both the liberal reformers and the Reaganite reactionaries have failed to make what I regard as a crucial distinction between the youthful nonviolent offender who usually deserves the liberal's tenderness and the cold-blooded violent criminal who should be put away for a long time and, especially when clearly guilty, should never be permitted to get out on the basis of technicalities.

Perhaps the most successful escape route for the violent who can afford to hire clever lawyers or have the luck to be assigned a Fortas is the insanity defense which has freed one dangerous criminal after another.

In 1989 David R. Peterson killed a nine-year-old girl by stabbing her thirty-four times. He was found not guilty by reason of insanity. He had previously made two other stabbing attacks but on each occasion had also been found not guilty because of insanity. As a result he was in a mental hospital, from which he escaped merely by strolling off the grounds. He went directly to a sporting goods shop, where he purchased a hunting knife. He then walked approximately a hundred yards from the store, seized nine-year-old Jessica Short, and proceeded to knife her to death.

In another appalling case, Edward Carter, Jr., of Washington, D.C. was charged with raping a thirteen-year-old girl but was also found not guilty by reason of insanity. Later, however, doctors concluded that he had been lying to them when he convinced them he was insane. The courts therefore had to release him—he hadn't been convicted of the crime, so he couldn't be imprisoned, and he wasn't insane, so he couldn't be kept in a mental hospital.

As with bail reform and other legacies of the *Gideon* decision, the excesses of the insanity defense are gradually being curbed by Congress and conservative courts. But occasionally the conservatives have gone too far. In a recent Supreme Court decision, for example, Justice Sandra Day

O'Connor ruled that a person can be held in jail for up to forty-eight hours without even being charged of a crime. It is safe to bet Ms. O'Connor has never spent an hour in jail and that she has no idea what a nightmare forty-eight hours would be for an innocent person.

But the clever lawyer can still make law that will spare the guilty. The Supreme Court ruled in 1990 that convicted criminals can avoid making restitution by declaring bankruptcy. Thus in states such as Florida and Texas, which permit even homes worth millions to be excluded from a bankrupt's assets, the criminal can avoid restitution to his victim simply by putting all his money into an expensive house.

If the Arnold, Fortas & Porter legacy was a mixed blessing to American criminal law, its effect on regulatory law was equally ambiguous. By the late seventies many observers were concluding that something had gone badly wrong with initially well-motivated regulation. A report on federal regulation made by a congressional oversight subcommittee concluded that the central characteristic of the nine regulatory agencies studied was their devotion "to the special interests of regulated industry and lack of sufficient concern for underreported interest"—that is, the public. The committee found that the Federal Power Commission and the Interstate Commerce Commission were the least effective of the nine agencies. The FPC, it noted, had "displayed a conscious indifference to the public beyond comparison with any other regulatory agency." As for the ICC, "Of all the agencies of government in Washington there is probably no worse example of federal regulation than the Interstate Commerce Commission," wrote Stephen Chapman in *The Washington Monthly*. Created in 1887 to regulate the nation's rail traffic and later given authority over waterways, pipelines, and highways as well, the commission had an almost spotless record, according to Chapman, of guarding and promoting the interests of the dominant companies and unions under its jurisdiction. It pushed rates above their normal levels, inflated the costs of doing business, contrived to shut out newcomers, encouraged inefficiency, and made a thorough mess of surface transportation in the United States. No agency ever cried out louder for abolishment than the ICC.

Such abuses produced a deregulatory movement that took root in the Carter administration and flourished under Ronald Reagan. In a few cases the movement effected desirable reform. One example was increased competition in the trucking industry. In airline and telephone business deregulation was a mixed blessing, leading to lower rates for long distance travel and long distance telephone calls, but to much higher rates for short plane trips and local phone service, including skyrocketing installation and repair costs for the average customer.

On health and safety issues, however, deregulation has been an unmitigated disaster. Trucking accidents increased; in just one year, 1983–84, they rose by 18 percent. As for oil tankers, although practically everyone knows about the *Exxon Valdez* oil spill off the coast of Alaska, few realize that, as the *Wall Street Journal* reported in 1990, "on two out of every three days on average, an oil tanker in U.S. water catches fire, explodes, collides with a dock or another ship, breaks apart, experiences mechanical failure, runs aground, or winds up in some other kind of accident."

In the wake of deregulation, OSHA (the Occupational Safety and Health Administration) stopped inspecting plants with good safety records, so many companies simply underreported accidents in order to maintain their records and keep inspectors out of their hair. The Reagan administration cut the staff of the Food and Drug Administration to the point where, as *Time* magazine reported in 1989, "Even regulated industries, fearing a low of consumer confidence, are demanding a stronger FDA."

But the most dramatic by far of the failures of deregulation involved the savings and loans.

In the late seventies, savings and loans began to lose

depositors to money market funds, which offered higher returns. The S&Ls could not compete because their own income, from which they paid interest to their depositors, was limited to their returns from low-interest, long-term mortgages, which were the only investment they were permitted to make. So Congress allowed the S&Ls to make other seemingly high-yield investments. Many of these were unsound, such as junk bonds or development of shopping centers or other commercial structures that should never have been built.

Congress also raised the amount of deposit insurance from $40,000 to $100,000 per account, but since it had decreased the rate the S&Ls had to pay for the insurance, the amount of liability the government took on rose while at the same time its income to fund the insurance decreased. When the S&Ls' investments went bad, the government had only the rapidly depleted insurance fund to pay them off. The resulting bailout will ultimately cost taxpayers hundreds of billions of dollars.

Congress's errors—all, by the way, enthusiastically advocated by S&L lobbyists—were compounded by the failure of regulators to keep track of what the S&Ls were doing with their new freedom to invest. And few of the regulators who knew about the bad investments that were being made had the courage to blow the whistle. In the notorious case of the Keating Five, the few courageous regulators were intimidated by powerful senators who, if they had not actually been bought off by Charles Keating, the wealthy chairman of Lincoln Savings & Loan, behaved as if they had.

To understand the regulatory mess, nothing is more important than remembering our principle that the system works less to serve the public's interest than the lawyers'. Take the "revolving door": A young lawyer just out of law school is hired by the Federal Trade Commission, where he gains expertise at the lower and middle levels. This makes him attractive to law firms that have clients with present or potential problems at the FTC. Once hired by such a firm, he will usually stay in private practice, but he might return to the FTC for a few years at a high level, say as director of the Bureau of Competition or as a commissioner. With that kind of experience, he can either start his own law firm or name his price with any of the major partnerships.

A 1986 article published in a Washington magazine describes an example. The story involved John Fedders, a high official in the Securities and Exchange Commission, who had been accused of beating his wife. Most of the story was purely personal, but buried in its back pages was a gem of insight into what motivates regulatory officials:

"The power that came with a government job appealed to him, but John told Charlotte what was most attractive was Washington's revolving-door tradition, whereby high-ranking government officials move into high-paying private industry jobs. He said he'd be able to springboard to at least a $300,000 salary with a Washington law firm."

John Jenkins described a classic case in *The Washington Monthly*:

"Federal Trade Commissioner Stephen A. Nye was in the job market. A San Francisco antitrust lawyer, Nye was cleaning out his desk at the FTC without any assurance, he told me, that a law firm would take him on. Had there been overtures from other firms? Not yet. I would be wrong to discuss employment with firms that had cases before the commission. Nye would take a West Coast vacation, then start looking around.

"Shortly before Nye left the FTC last year, I examined his phone and appointment logs, as well as those of his fellow commissioners. Of the outsiders who were listed as having visited Nye to discuss Commission matters (a perfectly legal practice), the name of Wallace Adair stood out. Adair, an attorney with the Washington law firm of Howrey, Simon, Baker & Murchison, represented Kennecott Copper Corporation, which was under an FTC order to sell off its

$1.2 billion Peabody Coal subsidiary. Kennecott had been dragging its feet. It wanted the FTC to reopen the case and amend its divestiture order and had retained Adair in an effort to achieve that result.

"Weeks later, after Nye left the FTC, I phoned him at home. 'He's not here,' said the voice at the other end of the line. 'You can reach him at Howrey & Simon. He started there yesterday.'

"'He's probably in Mr. Adair's office,' the law firm's receptionist added cheerfully, when I called.'"

One consequence of the revolving door is that the large private law firm develops an expertise in manipulating the regulatory agencies, with the result that it usually succeeds in either defeating regulatory action against its clients or at least mitigating any unhappy consequences of those actions. Often delay will serve the client just as well as outright victory. And when the potential for delay in the regulatory agencies is joined with that in the courts, the possibilities are practically limitless.

Take, for example, the case of the El Paso Natural Gas Company. In 1959, after lengthy proceedings at the commission level, the Federal Power Commission approved the merger of El Paso with the Pacific Northwest Pipeline Company. The Justice Department appealed, however, and the case eventually made its way to the Supreme Court, which in 1962 ruled that the FPC should not have approved the merger. El Paso's lawyers were masters at legal foot-dragging, so it was not surprising that in 1964 the Supreme court again ordered El Paso to divest Pacific Northwest "without delay."

Then El Paso's lawyers persuaded the federal judge overseeing the divestiture to adopt a plan so favorable to El Paso that outraged consumers brought the case to the Supreme Court yet again, in 1967. The case returned to the Supreme Court two more times before finally being disposed of—and then only after the late Tommy Corcoran, the famous New Dealer turned lobbyist, had made personal approaches to two justices, Hugo Black and William Brennan, in an effort to get a rehearing for El Paso.

Why would a lawyer of Corcoran's standing engage in such scandalous attempts to lobby Supreme Court justices? The reason may well have been the large amount of money involved. Certainly money was the motive behind one major Washington firm's advice to a potential client with an antitrust problem. The story, as told to me by a lawyer who has worked for the firm, was that the client was told his legal situation was hopeless—he was doomed to lose the case—but the firm could stretch matters out for ten years or so, meaning the client could go on making money doing whatever he was doing wrong for those ten years. The client was asked whether he would be willing to pay $500,000 to $1 million a year for the legal fees such a delay would require. The answer: "Of course."

Here was a client who knew he was wrong and a law firm that knew he was wrong. Yet they were both willing to delay the triumph of the public interest for ten years. That may have been bad for the public, but what about the $5 million to $10 million it cost the client? Wouldn't that hurt? Hardly—legal fees are tax deductible.

Mickey Kaus, then of *The Washington Monthly*, now of the *New Republic,* once asked an attorney for the Environmental Protection Agency for an example of an average delay. He was told about a case in which the EPA had spent two years haggling with the state of Idaho over the amount of sulfur dioxide a steel mill was releasing into the atmosphere. After taking testimony from every scientist and engineer in sight, the EPA ruled that the mill's sulfur dioxide emission had to be reduced by 82 percent. The state thereupon took the case to federal court, which after another two years' wait sent it back to the EPA so it could start all over again. The EPA lawyer concluded: "I just think that's life. I don't think it's something that has to be reformed."

But it *can* be reformed. The secret is to outlaw the revolving door. Some observers contend that such a reform would be too costly because it would deprive the government of the services of all those bright young lawyers who want to get rich. I think the opposite. We don't want lawyers who see a short period of government employment as something they can exploit for private gain later in life. We want lawyers in government who are there because they are excited by the prospect of serving the public interest.

But because lawyers make so much money out of the system as it is, even those who advocate reform usually want to do so by adding legal procedures. The most ironic reform idea of all is Ralph Nader's proposal to establish a consumer protection agency whose lawyers would intervene on behalf of the public in proceedings of the existing regulatory agencies—the same agencies that were originally established to protect the public.

In a book called *The Genteel Populists,* Simon Lazarus, a former public interest lawyer who went on to join Arnold & Porter, concludes that the real hope of regulatory reform lies in making the regulators' decisions easier to appeal in the courts. You have to be a true believer in the adversary system to think that more of it is the answer. In fact, the adversary system is itself central to the problem. What it does is pit two sides against one another, with self-interest motivating the contending lawyers less toward the pursuit of truth and justice than toward the pursuit of victory.

The way lawyers view truth and justice is suggested by this advice from the book *How to Cross-examine Witnesses Successfully*: "No matter how clear, how logical, how concise, or how honest a witness may be or make his testimony appear, there is always some way, if you are ingenious enough, to cast suspicion on it, to weaken its effect." Ann Strick has described the American system of justice as a modern version of the medieval trial by battle, in which the strongest won. The richest win now because they can hire the brightest lawyers. Between the lawyers stands a judge, who in the main tradition of American law is not a seeker after truth and justice but a referee who aims only to ensure that the combatants obey the rules. This means, among other things, that he does not intervene to protect the poor man with a bad lawyer from the rich man with a good one.

It is possible for disputes to be handled otherwise—by judges who seek justice and truth, as do many English jurists and as did Judge Sirica in the Watergate case, and who take responsibility for protecting each party's rights, as some small claims courts now do. It is also possible for disputes to be settled by mediators who try to find solutions that are fair to both sides and that enable the parties to leave the dispute as friends rather than enemies.

The adversary system is cruelest in divorce cases. For the sake of their children, parents need to go forward in life with mutual respect and affection; instead they are encouraged to blame one another for what went wrong in their marriage and often leave the courtroom with hatred in their hearts.

The auto accident is the most absurd of all adversary proceedings. In most cases, what happened was an *accident.* If any one did it deliberately or recklessly, he would be prosecuted as a criminal, but, with no one really to blame, or with both parties sharing responsibility, the adversary system says you have to prove that it was all the other guy's fault, or in some jurisdictions that he was more at fault or that he had a "last clear chance" to prevent the wreck.

Auto accident cases inflate insurance premiums for everyone and cause endless delays in payments to the injured. For this reason a number of states have adopted no-fault systems for settling personal injury claims arising from auto accidents. But an attempt to get such a system enacted nationally was defeated in the Senate in 1976. Intensive lobbying by the American Trial Lawyers Association (the fellows the senators need at campaign time) brought it down. Even in the states that have no-fault provisions, the lawyers' lobby has watered it down to the point that the savings are not nearly what they could be.

In China, disputes of this type (there they usually involved bicycles) are settled by mediation. In the seventies our own government sponsored experimental "neighborhood justice centers" in three cities, where mediators handled consumer, landlord, employer, and family problems. Bearing in mind the time the regular legal system takes to handle disputes, it is interesting to note that hearings at the Kansas City center usually took just two hours. And it took only thirteen days (on the average) from the time a case was filed for it to be heard. Reagan's budget cutters, in their inimitable manner, did away with the program.

If the government really wanted to save money by getting rid of unnecessary lawsuits, it would expand rather than shut down such experiments. It would also make two other changes. First, as Jonathan Alter has suggested, litigants should be charged a "user's fee" in civil cases (such as contract disputes) involving wealthy parties arguing over exclusively private matters. Since 90 percent of us never use the courts in our entire lives, why are we paying the full cost of putting on trials for wealthy adversaries?

The second reform is to adopt a "loser pays" provision. The California Legislature has provided for mandatory arbitration of all cases involving amounts less than $15,000. If either party is unhappy with an arbitrator's decision the case can go on to trial, but the loser can be ordered to pay the other party's fees for both the trial and the arbitration. In England, the courts can compel the losing party to pay the winner's legal costs without California's limitation on the amount involved. Probably no single reform would do more to reduce the amount of litigation than the adoption of this English rule in all American courts. Then only those who were confident of the rightness of their cause would go to court.

Why do most American lawyers oppose adopting the English rule? It would mean less business, which brings us back to where we started: The American legal system serves lawyers, not the people.

7.

CONGRESS

The most striking feature of the life of a member of Congress is its hectic jumble of votes, meetings, appointments, and visits from folks from back home who just drop by. From an 8:00 A.M. breakfast conference with a group of union leaders, a typical morning will take him to his office around 9:00, where the waiting room is filled with people who want to see him. (If the congressman is unlucky enough to be new and assigned to the overcrowded Longworth Building, the waiting room will also function as an office for as many as ten members of his staff. The overall effect can only be compared to the Marx Brothers' cabin in *A Night at the Opera*.)

From 9:00 until 10:30 or so, he will try to give the impression that he is devoting his entire attention to a businessman from his state with a tax problem; to a delegation of constituents protesting their town's loss of air service; to a voter and his three children, who are in Washington and want to say hello; and to a couple of staff members whose morale will collapse if they don't have five minutes alone with him to go over essential business. As he strives to project one-on-one sincerity to all those people, he is fielding phone calls at the rate of one every five minutes and checking a press release that has to get out in time to make the afternoon papers in his district.

He leaves this madhouse to go to a committee meeting, accompanied by his legislative aide, who tries to brief him on the business before the committee along the way. The meeting started at 10:00, so once there he struggles to catch the thread of questioning while a staff member whispers in his ear. And so the day continues.

Ironically, despite all this activity, most members of Congress feel a sense of isolation most of the time. The people they see—constituents, lobbyists, reporters—usually want something, which means the congressman must be guarded in his relationships with them. And there is less relaxed comradeship among members than there used to be. In the old days when sessions were shorter, members left their families back home and spent their evenings together. The House Ways and Means Committee used to have dinner one night a week at a restaurant in downtown Washington. These were also the days of unrecorded legislative action, when much of the voting on the floor was done in ways that protected the public's right not to know where its representatives stood. Back then many a congressional friendship was cemented by an exchange of votes. Such mutual favors are possible today only when the recorded vote is certain not to damage either congressman's standing with his constituents.

Now that the bonds forged through after-hours socializing and exchanging mutual favors are much less common, there are fewer close friendships among members. A member is probably closest to his staff. They truly care about him, at least in the sense that their jobs and futures depend on his performance and eventual reelection. But this identity of interests does not relieve him of anxiety about what they, should they someday choose to leave his employ, might say about what he has said or done in an unguarded moment. This is the main reason politicians have few close relationships of any kind. As Ross Baker of Rutgers has pointed out, "The establishment of a personal friendship involves a degree of risk, for . . . there is the likelihood of self-revelation, the exposure of innermost thoughts, the exchange of confidences, the laying bare of personal problems."

The arrangement of offices on Capitol Hill tends to reinforce members' sense of isolation. Each senator or representative, with his staff, occupies a suite of offices set off from those of his colleagues. (Although his case may have been extreme, it is said that the late John McClellan, a senator from Arkansas for over thirty years, never set foot in the office of another senator.) To be sure, other members are encountered in committee meetings and on the floor, but in each place the focus is necessarily on the business at hand. They can meet in the Senate or House dining rooms, but there one has the feeling that everyone is "on," in the theatrical sense of the word: performing and posturing; wondering who that familiar and possibly important person is with Senator Y; asking himself whether he should rise to greet the national committeeman who is passing by; and often, even after he has been a member for years, being almost as awed by his surroundings as the average visitor.

More often than not the average member of the House, when first elected, is not a prominent citizen. Often he has reached his mid-thirties without having achieved conspicuous success (perhaps, to his credit because of his pursuit of good causes instead of private gain), and is ready to gamble to make it, to pursue the long shot of defeating an incumbent congressman. But if he runs a particularly effective campaign, or runs against a particularly ineffective opponent, or happens to run in a "tidal wave" year (1964, 1974, and 1980), he wins the gamble. Having kept his spirits up during the campaign with thoughts like "Well, even if I lose, the publicity will help my law practice," he now finds himself a congressman.

Usually a newly elected congressman is so impressed by his opponent's misfortune that his first resolution is to make sure a similar tragedy does not befall him. And this helps explain the first and fundamental rule of life on the Hill: Each member is concerned above all else with getting reelected. Nothing will help you understand Congress better than the reelection imperative. Do you wonder why the average staff member spends four-fifths of his time on constituent service and one-fifth on legislation? Service to constituents tends to be most solicitous in cases involving generous campaign contributors. Senator Alan Cranston was so zealous in his efforts on behalf of an S&L magnate, Charles Keating, that he was actually formally reprimanded by his colleagues in 1991, but this was a rare exception to congressional tolerance of favoritism for rich constituents.

Are you puzzled by the fact that Congress does little to remedy those defects in the bureaucracy against which it constantly rails? The reason is that Congress itself has a stake in bureaucratic ineptitude.

As the political scientist Morris Fiorina has pointed out, the more bureaucrats wrong the public, the more favors congressmen can do for their constituents in righting these wrongs—or rather, in appearing to right them. That word *appearing* is the key to understanding the congressional world of make-believe.

Suppose that your local postmaster spends his time reading his mail rather than seeing that yours is delivered, and the poor mail service is hurting your business. You're mad as hell, and you write your congressman to say you're not going to take it anymore. He promptly and efficiently forwards your complaint to the Postal Service, which responds that nothing can be done because your postmaster is protected by civil service laws. Your congressman then promptly forwards you a copy of the Postal Service's letter and puts you on his mailing list—after which you henceforth regularly receive (allowing ten days for delivery) the *Congressional Record*, which contains somewhere in its multitudinous pages the congressman's denunciations of postal inefficiency. "Well, I guess nothing can be done," you sigh, "but my congressman certainly seems to have done his best"—and you then resolve to vote for him next time around.

Besides taking care of—or appearing to take care of—specific constituents, getting reelected also involves avoiding any action that might antagonize a sizable interest group. Since most members have nightmares about losing by ten votes, a group with eleven members can have influence if they make clear they feel strongly about their views. This is the basic reason why lobbies run the American government today.

The growing power of lobbies is best illustrated by the tendency of Congress to organize itself into interest group caucuses such as the well-known Black Caucus. But have you heard of the Footwear Caucus? There is one. There is also a Sweetener Caucus, a Soybean Caucus, and a [Ball] Bearing Caucus. My favorite is the Mushroom Caucus.

Interest groups have always been with us, but they used to operate within coalitions called the Democratic and Republican parties. As long as these groups functioned within a party, they were compelled to compromise with the other groups under the party's umbrella. But as first federal and then state and local governments embraced civil service and deprived them of the patronage that had glued them together, the parties declined and the power and assertiveness of lobbies grew—along with the ability to enforce their demands through campaign contributions.

It's easier for a member than a challenger to get contributions. The lobbyist knows that the odds favor incumbents. Congress has helped make the odds by enacting measure after measure designed to keep incumbents in office. For instance, they have access to television facilities in the capital where they can tape programs for stations in their districts. They also have free mailing privileges. Each time a member sends a newsletter to his constituents, he not only has the staff's work in preparing it paid by the taxpayer but, assuming a typical mailing to two hundred thousand constituents, gets a postal subsidy of $58,000.

Congress takes great pains to avoid reminding voters that they themselves finance such mailings. The postage-free (franked) envelopes used for mailings usually bear only the member's signature. Once, however, a staff error resulted in the appearance of the phrase POSTAGE PAID BY CONGRESS under the facsimile signatures. But Representative Morris Udall was soon able to reassure his colleagues:

"I'm happy to report that the House committee on the Post Office and Civil Service today added a repealer of this unfortunate goof to a Senate-passed bill, S. 2315, and that the bill is expected to be on the next Consent Calendar.

"Members who are concerned about using envelopes with the new language might consider withholding orders for new supplies of franked envelopes for a few days until the repealer can be signed into law.

"I personally regret this error and any difficulty it might have caused."

S. 2315, as amended, passed the House by unanimous consent, and the Senate passed it two weeks later. It is reassuring to know that our Congress is capable of rapid action in a genuine emergency.

The ingenuity of congressmen in finding ways to tap the public till in the interest of their own reelection is perhaps best illustrated by this editorial from the *Washington Post* about former congressman Ted Risenhoover:

"The Risenhoover campaign committee has bought television time to air . . . a half-hour version of the official Air Force film of this year's Flag Day observance in the House. As edited by Rep. Risenhoover at his own expense (a modest $650, compared with the $5000-or-so the Air Force spent to produce the film), this epic documentary includes an inspirational address by evangelist Oral Roberts, whose headquarters is in Tulsa. (Risenhoover is from Oklahoma.) But the dramatic climax is a reading of "I Am an American" by the chairman of the House Flag Day Committee, backed up by the Air Force's Singing Sergeants and band. Do we have to tell you who is this year's chairman of the House Flag Day Committee?"

After wondering how it came to pass that the air force had filmed this minor event, the *Post* continued:

". . . it was not a one-time favor to a two-term congressman. Instead it has become routine over the years for the services to supply a band and a camera crew for the House's annual Flag Day show. The Air Force simply got the call this year.

"The film is quietly handed over to the Flag Day chairman, and his office distributes it. Mr. Risenhoover thinks highly of this service; he shared last year's movie—in which he was shown making a patriotic speech—with some 200 groups in his district."

Does the senator or representative, you must be beginning to wonder, ever spend any time on legislation? Yes, he does, and we're coming to that. But first you should realize that his concern with legislation is often less with its substance than with its potential effect on his campaign for reelection. There is no better illustration of this than a resolution guided by Representative Romano L. Mazzoli through the Ninety-second Congress Democratic Club. It read:

"WHEREAS, in the 92nd Congress the Democratic Party enjoys a majority of the membership of the House of Representatives; and

"WHEREAS, it is in the best interests of the people of the United States that this majority be maintained or expanded in future elections; and

"WHEREAS, the development of a substantial legislative record is a major assistance in reelection campaigns;

"Be It Resolved By The 92nd Congress Democratic Club:

"That the Democratic Leadership of the House of Representatives of the 92nd Congress is requested and urged to develop a program whereby first-term Democratic Members of Congress receive advance notice of important legislation likely to receive Party support and thus likely to become law, and that such interested Members be afforded an opportunity to join in the sponsorship of such legislation in order to compile a substantial legislative record on which to run for re-election."

Before we get to members' work on legislation we should note other major uses of their time. Part of the motivation in seeking office is the chance to lead the life they imagined was led by important men in Washington. This involves lunches in fancy restaurants with celebrities, weekends at sporting events and hunting lodges, dinners with the social and financial elite, and in general just being with people who give a warm sense of importance. And then there is traveling—trips at the taxpayers' expense to such essential events as meetings of the Interparliamentary Union, which usually manages to hold its conventions in places like Geneva or Lisbon.

The late Marvella Bayh's autobiography makes clear that she and her husband, Birch, the former senator from Indiana, enjoyed the pleasures of Interparliamentary travel three times in just one ten-month period. The grandest was a three-week "study trip" to seven Asian countries, but there was also a jaunt to Monaco and an excursion to Paris. Indeed, Mrs. Bayh recalls her first words on hearing from her father that Birch had been elected to the Senate: "Daddy, do you know what his means? It means some day I may go to Europe!"

Congressional travel delegations (designated CODELs in State Department cable-ese) include not only members of the House and Senate but members' staff and spouses, or— what many taxpayers do not realize—if a spouse is not going, other relatives such as mothers, fathers, brothers, and sisters. Although the use of government aircraft requires an initial commitment of ten members to go on a trip, such commitments can be canceled just beforehand. Often, they are made simply as favors to the one or two members who actually want to go with their entourages of staff and family.

At each stop, the State Department arranges entertainment and sightseeing and provides a "control room" to provide local currency and alcoholic refreshment around the clock. Air accommodations include first-class seating and military stewards who cook fresh meals, billing the passengers only for the cost of the ingredients.

Congress offers other opportunities for recreation to its members. The powerful have hideaway offices that provide a place for solitary contemplation or for entertaining attractive members of the opposite sex. There are saunas, gymnasiums, and swimming pools; free drinks are available in the offices of the secretary of the Senate and certain other congressional officials. And, of course, there is free parking.

The House has shut down that nice bank that kept cashing checks even when members didn't have a dime left in their accounts, but these other perks remain although even they are endangered by the reformist zeal that was engendered by the exposes during the spring of 1992.

• At National Airport, the public spaces closest to the terminals—just on the far side of the free ones provided to Congress—cost $20 a day.

• Senators have free use of indoor tennis and basketball courts that private clubs charge $1,500 a year for.

• Congressmen get free health care that costs the taxpayer $2,794 for each member. And this doesn't count the additional free care available at both Walter Reed Army Medical Center and the Bethesda Naval Medical Center.

• Studios where senators can produce videotapes of themselves to send to television or radio stations cost the taxpayers $17,000 per member and give incumbents an incalculable advantage over challengers, who not only have to pay for such facilities but rarely enjoy the convenience of having the studio just a few steps away.

• A club sandwich in the subsidized House and Senate

dining rooms costs over one-third less than it does at the closest comparable restaurant, which also happens to be considerably less spacious than the congressional restaurants.

On Capitol Hill, parking costs the average person $135 to $200 a month. So when a senator proposed that congressmen and their staffs pay from $10 to $50 a month, depending on their incomes, it seemed the most modest of reforms. The congressmen would still be getting a bargain. If anyone didn't want to pay he could use public transportation and save energy. All in all, an irresistible case.

When the vote came in the Senate, however, it lost sixty-five to twenty-eight. Among those voting for free parking were most conservatives, who say they oppose government handouts, and most environmentalists, who supposedly support energy conservation.

Congress does do important work. Enough members combine idealism and intelligence—there were, after all, twenty-eight nays on that parking vote—to make them and their generally younger and even more idealistic staffs the most impressive pool of talent in Washington. They take their responsibilities seriously. These duties include determining the need for legislation, writing laws, and investigating how they are carried out.

Sometimes there is conflict between these legislative and investigative functions. Congressman A, while diligently pursuing investigative leads, may find himself exposing defects in Congressman B's favorite program. This means B will be less likely to support bills sponsored by A.

Bills are introduced by members on their own initiative or at the suggestion of the executive branch or of a lobbyist for the private sector. Once introduced they are referred to committees, which is where most of the substantive work of Congress takes place. In 1990 the House had 172 committees and subcommittees—which meant, among other things, that 172 of the 262 Democrats then in the House could be chairmen and enjoy the power and publicity attendant on that role. The largest committees are Appropriations, with 59 members; and Public Works and Transportation, 59. Except for Rules, Ways and Means, and Appropriations, which are exclusive assignments, a House member may serve on one major committee and one other less important committee. In the Senate, where the committee load is heavier, a typical member might be on as many as three committees and six subcommittees. The total number of committees and subcommittees for the House and the Senate stood at 283 in 1992. There were only thirty-eight in 1947.

Until the trend was arrested, the size of committee staffs had been increasing dramatically in recent years. In the House, for example, there were 634 persons on committee staffs in 1967. By 1990 that figure had tripled. The main reason for this growth was that Congress no longer trusted the executive branch to provide it with accurate information. Vietnam, Watergate, and Iran-contra combined to make people on the Hill wary of what they were being told by those downtown. More congressional staffers—by 1990, the total number of Capitol Hill employees had risen to 24,000—were hired to check the facts alleged by the administration and to search for the unhappy news that the executive branch so often omits from its reports. Congress is aided in this work by the General Accounting Office, an organization that has responded to the lessons of Vietnam, Watergate, and the savings and loan scandals by developing an investigative potential considerably beyond the fiscal audit function to which it was once largely confined. Still, like its fellow investigators from the press and the congressional committees, the GAO tends to spend more time looking for fraud and illegality than in appraising program effectiveness—whether the programs Congress enacted actually work and if not, why—which is what Congress most needs to know.

These problems were highlighted in an article that John Heilemann wrote for the July/August 1989 issue of *The Washington Monthly* entitled "Congress's Watch Dog:

Mostly It Still Goes for the Capillaries." Heilemann also observed that "more often than not GAO arrives on the scene in the aftermath, like some super State Farm agent, clucking over the mess and adding up the bill." A conspicuous example of this kind of dereliction in the eighties was its failure to spot the scandal at HUD while it was developing and could have been stopped before the losses became horrendous.

GAO reports also tend to be dull, which of course limits their audience and effectiveness. In this respect, the GAO might look for a model to the Office of Technology Assessment, which evaluates technological matters for Congress and whose reports are often both literate and lively as well as candid.

One reform of recent years has been the establishment of the Congressional Budget Office and the House and Senate Budget committees. Before these committees existed, Congress had no way to evaluate the budget priorities given by the executive branch. Furthermore, it had no effective way to discipline itself on expenditures. Now, by budget resolutions, it establishes targets in May and final ceilings in September. The Congressional Budget Office gives Congress a means, unfortunately still underused, of assessing executive branch assertions that this weapons program will cost X dollars or that tax measure will produce Y dollars.

In another reform motivated by Vietnam, Congress passed the War Powers Act in 1973, the first time in history that it had defined and limited the president's power to make war.

These measures, however, do not begin to make up for the powers that Congress has lost in the last half century. Congress itself has been largely responsible for this decline through its enthusiastic adoption of two "reforms"—delegation of rule-making power and revenue sharing. Delegation became popular during the New Deal, when Congress got in the habit of setting up agencies to solve problems while giving them only the vaguest of instructions. The National Labor Relations Board, for example, was established to ban "unfair labor practices"; the Securities and Exchange Commission, to prohibit "manipulative or deceptive devices" in the sale of stocks and bonds. When the agencies wrote "rules" in an attempt to give substance to these platitudes, the rules had the force of law—except that they were laws Congress had never voted on. In effect, Congress repeatedly gave away a sizable chunk of power to the unelected civil servants who staff federal agencies.

Revenue sharing is a more recent innovation. As initiated by President Nixon, the idea was to transfer power away from the unaccountable federal agency officials to state and local officials, who were presumably closer to the people. In fact, however, revenue sharing—and the growth, now stopped, of other federal subsidies to state and local governments—gave those governments the wherewithal to finance their own imitations of federal agencies and the federal civil service. So the effect had once again been to shift power away from a potentially accountable Congress to unaccountable bureaucrats—although this time the bureaucrats were in the state capitols and city halls rather than in Washington.

As a result, Congress today is largely a reactive body. The Founding Fathers intended that Congress would make policy and the president, if he did not use his veto, would execute it. The actual process, however, is that a lobby or the administration proposes legislation; Congress assents to it (often with amendments), or rejects it; and then the executive branch and the states "implement" it.

In many areas where congressional assent is necessary, it is almost automatic. The only time since 1959 a cabinet nominee has been turned down by the Senate was when George Bush's nomination of John Tower as secretary of defense was rejected. As one staff member explained, nominees "can be crummy, mediocre, not qualified, even in industry's pocket, and if they haven't done anything criminal, they're approved. You almost have to be found with one finger in the cookie jar to get rejected."

Even when Congress *wants* to carry out its duties, there are obstacles. One is the way it is organized. For example, responsibility for federal pension programs is divided among nineteen Senate and House committees and subcommittees. Jurisdiction over energy legislation is even more fragmented, with twenty-five committees and subcomittees involved.

Another obstacle to congressional effectiveness is the communication gap between the executive and legislative branches. The culture of the Hill is vastly different from the culture of bureaucracy. While both cultures place a high value on holding on to one's job—on surviving in Washington—the congressman who has to risk all on the throw-of-the-dice of elective politics does not easily empathize with the bureaucrat, who seldom has to risk anything. And the bureaucrat, of course, regards the congressman as a "politician," which, in the lexicon of the civil service, is removed by only the most delicate shade of meaning from "crook."

The fact that the bureaucrat and the congressman inhabit different cultures is most evident when an executive branch witness appears before a congressional committee. Unless the witness has had some political experience—and usually this is true of only a few people at the top of an agency—he is almost certain to be defensive and to be primarily concerned with protecting himself and his agency. He is not forthright. When I worked in the executive branch I felt it was my duty to conceal from Congress any fact that might reflect adversely on my agency. The congressmen, on the other hand, were usually ill prepared (remember what their typical day is like) and seldom asked me the right questions. When they did, it was seemingly accidental, and they failed to ask the right follow-up questions.

Congress seldom requires executive branch witnesses to testify under oath. Ninety percent of such testimony is not under oath, and as a result is usually removed from precise truth by degrees varying from the subtlest unconscious nuance to the grossest and most deliberate distortion. The danger of all this is that, unless ways can be found to remind executive branch witnesses that they and the Congress work for the same United States and that it is not in the interest of the country for there to be a lack of candor between the branches of its government, it is possible that we will end up with another giant bureaucracy on the Hill to check the one downtown.

We have already discussed the growth of committee staffs. The same thing has happened to the staffs of individual congressmen. In 1979, Courtney Pace retired after thirty-five years as a staff member for former senator James Eastland. When Pace first joined there were but three other persons on the staff and the total annual payroll for all was $11,000. When he retired, twenty-four employees worked in Eastland's office in Washington and eight or nine more in his home-state offices. The payroll had grown to $525,000. By 1990, the payrolls for each of the senators from Mississippi exceeded $1 million. Members of the House have staffs almost as large. Each, regardless of seniority or committee assignment, is allotted eighteen employees.

Staff members have little interest in blowing the whistle on this situation. Instead they are dedicated to convincing their bosses that their work is essential. Just as the caseworker—the staff member who handles constituent problems—doesn't want Agency X reformed because its misdeeds supply half his work, the legislative assistant doesn't want the congressman to have other sources of information about legislation. Every staff member is tempted to be an Iago, contributing to the member's isolation.

One of the great truths of Washington life little known by the folks back home is the power of congressional staff members. Norman Dicks, who was elected to the House after spending eight years as an aide to Senator Warren Magnuson, was subsequently quoted by Martin Tolchin of

the *New York Times* as saying, "People asked me how I felt
about being elected to Congress, and I told them I never
thought I'd give up that much power voluntarily." At the
time of the death of Laurence Woodworth, who had been
staff director of the Joint Committee on Internal Revenue
for fourteen years, Representative Al Ullman, then the committee chairman, said, "In his quaint way he was as much
an influence in shaping tax policy in this country as any
committee chairman or treasury secretary or president in
recent memory." Similarly, until he resigned, Harley Dirks
of the House Appropriations Committee staff was known as
the man to see on anything affecting labor, health, education, or welfare appropriations. And Richard Perle, when
he was assistant to Senator Henry Jackson, was the most
influential force on Capitol Hill on arms control and disar-
mament issues.

Congressional staff members, like Supreme Court clerks,
are a great example of subordinate power. No one knows
this better than the lobbyists, who in a recent survey rated
congressional staffs as their number-one lobbying target (by
contrast, the White House ranked sixth). The member of
Congress himself is well aware of this power. He wants
bright, aggressive people on his staff. This means that, in
order to keep them satisfied, he will, at least occasionally,
have to introduce the bills they want enacted and ask the
questions they want raised. Former senator John Culver
explained to Elizabeth Drew:

". . . You get a bright staff person who works for months
on something in the subcommittee that he's particularly
interested in, and finally you don't want to disappoint him
or her, and you say, 'Go ahead,' only to regret it later
because you find yourself involved in something that you
don't have sufficient interest in, and spending your energy
and political capital on frustrating and unsatisfying efforts."

The congressman can become too dependent on his staff.
There was, for example, the time Senator James Sasser lost

his place in a statement he was making to the Government Affairs Committee. His aide was, unfortunately, seated several feet away, so everyone could hear Sasser's agonized whisper, "What comes next?"

If the staff's work is bad, this dependence can leave the congressman out on a very long limb, as was illustrated in the Carter administration by Senator Charles Percy's questioning of OMB director Bert Lance about use of his company plane. Of over a hundred trips by Lance to his vacation home at Sea Island, Percy asked about one on February 5, to which Lance was able to reply, "That was to the American Banking Association convention that was held at Sea Island." Percy then questioned Lance about a trip he had made to Warm Springs, asking if the nearest airport to Warm Springs wasn't at Lynchburg, Virginia. Lance pointed out that to Georgians, Warm Springs means the one in Georgia, not the one in Virginia.

Congressional wives take delight in pointing out that kind of error to their husbands. Hostility bordering on open warfare is typical of spouse-staff relations. The wife who lives through her husband—they are less common in this era of liberated women, but they still exist—often secretly thinks of herself as "the real senator." Since the husband's administrative assistant (or "AA," as this staff member is called on the Hill) usually thinks *he* is the real senator, conflict is practically inevitable. On the other hand, the person most victimized by the congressman's life is the wife who seeks an honest relationship of mutual support and respect.

The typical day we began to describe at the opening of this chapter usually ends around 11:30 P.M. as the congressman leaves an embassy party, at which he has been hustling as if it was a key precinct on election eve. He is too tired to talk about any but the most trivial matters—too tired, usually, to do anything but fall into bed and go to sleep. This is why most congressional marital disputes—that is, the really serious ones—are faced only on vacations. As Marvella Bayh wrote: "All those bottled-up complaints most people deal with and work through on a day-to-day basis suddenly surface. For us, there had been no day-to-day basis in the six years we had been in Washington, except for vacations. Then the bottle came uncorked."

Except for such rare occasions, then, the congressman's isolation is complete. He doesn't even communicate with his wife. He shakes hands with hundreds of people every day, but he really *talks* to no one.

This lack of genuine relationships with other human beings is characteristic of the unreality of Capitol Hill. If the reporters covering Congress are wrapped in the cocoon we described in Chapter 2, the congressmen themselves are even more insulated. The Capitol and its six satellite office buildings constitute a self-contained world connected by underground passageways that permit the congressman to avail himself of the services of barbers, nurses, credit unions, travel bureaus, cafeterias, and restaurants without once having to encounter life outside. One congressman managed to turn his office into an apartment and lived there around the clock.

It is easy for those enveloped in this cocoon to imagine that it is the real world—to think, for example, that they are affecting reality by enacting legislation when all they are doing is passing a bill that may well, depending on how it is carried out by the administration, have no effect at all. This is the ultimate make-believe.

The make-believe could be eliminated if Congress systematically traced its laws through the bureaucracy to see what finally happened after their enactment. Did a law solve the problem it was designed to meet? Or should it be amended or repealed in light of experience? This kind of follow-up, ironically called "legislative oversight" in the jargon of Congress, is one of the most neglected of congressional duties. The reason for the neglect is simple: There are no votes in oversight. The people simply do not understand its importance.

Even when there is oversight, it is likely to be perfunctory. Often survival networks are involved, and the committee chairman does not want to be hard on an old friend. Even when survival networks are not a factor, key committee members may perceive an identity of interest with the executive department concerned. For example, the chairman whose district's prosperity depends on defense contracts is not likely to be a severe cross-examiner of witnesses from the Department of Defense. He knows his own survival at the polls would be endangered by excessive zeal as an overseer, zeal that might anger the DOD and cause cancellation of his district's contracts. In other words, the average congressman knows that effective oversight may lose votes. Since he also knows of no sign, not even the faintest indication, that the public understands the importance of skillful oversight and might reward him for it at the polls, the ultimate villain behind make-believe on Capitol Hill is the ignorance of the people and the sloth and ineptitude of those who are charged with informing and educating them.

8.

THE
WHITE HOUSE

The White House is even more insulated from reality than is Capitol Hill, replete with comforts and privileges not usually available to the rest of us. Senior staff members have woodburning fireplaces for the winter and fresh flowers on their desks in the summer. (Because John Sununu had allergies, his flowers were silk.) They also have reserved parking places for their own cars and chauffeur-driven White House automobiles to take them to lunch and meetings around town. They can go to Camp David when Bill Clinton is out of town. When they accompany Clinton on trips, they fly on Air Force One with service and accommodations much superior to first class on commercial airlines. If they lunch at work, it's in the White House mess, where excellent meals are served by Filipino stewards below cost. They can use the White House swimming pool, tennis court, health club, medical facilities, gym, and hair salon. They can sit in the presidential box at the Kennedy Center and view movies free in the White House theater. The comfort and convenience of the president himself comes first in the use of all these facilities. He is the most insulated of all.

This insulation can be lessened or compounded by a president's personality. Bill Clinton seems determined to be more accessible than those who preceded him, and he may decide to eliminate some of the perquisites that have separated previous White House occupants from the rest of us. Both Reagan and Bush seemed to take great pleasure in their splendid isolation, which was compounded by their preference for the company of the economic and social elite—in Reagan's case, rich Californians; in Bush's, his old Skull and Bones crowd.

Jimmy Carter was not from that elite, but he was even more isolated. When he celebrated his first Christmas in office by giving a reception for members of the White House staff and their families, he provided nothing to eat or drink—not even potato chips and Coke—and to top it off, neither he nor any other member of the First Family bothered to show up. As this story suggests, Carter did not have a warm personal relationship with most of his staff. Only a handful saw him socially or, more important, on any business other than that which fitted within the stated duties of their positions on the organization charts. He talked to his speech writers only about speeches, to his economics adviser only about economics; even then, communication was largely in writing. His employees were not encouraged to make suggestions outside their nominal subject areas; he did not invite assistants to argue cases before him, hearing the strengths and weaknesses of each side's views. Instead he spent long hours alone, reading memoranda, and making check marks to indicate the recommendations that he approved. Within each department or agency his personal contacts were usually limited to its head and perhaps one or two others. He had not chosen the people just below the cabinet level—those who actually have their hands on the controls of much of the government—and maintained few contacts with them. Because of this isolation he heard very little dissent, seldom received the critical stimulation lively oral argument can provide, and had the personal loyalty of astonishingly few members of his administration.

What difference does such isolation make to the country? For one thing, bad decisions result when there is no one to point out to the President the holes in what is proposed by the adviser with responsibility for whatever issue is at hand. During George Bush's administration, the most important example of decision making by too small a group was the Gulf War. Key decisions were discussed by only six men: Bush, Brent Scowcroft, Dick Cheney, John Sununu, Colin Powell, and James Baker—and sometimes just by Bush and Scowcroft. The result was a failure to explore alternatives thoroughly. For example, only once during the meetings of this group was the case made for economic sanctions instead of war, and it was argued only briefly, by Colin Powell, before being brushed aside by Bush.

Carter permitted all officials whose interests might be affected by a proposal to send him written comments about it before the proposal landed on his desk. But there was still little face-to-face argument in front of or with Carter, and there was no involvement at all of many bright people on issues that might have been completely outside their formal sphere of responsibility but about which they could have had something helpful to say. The result was policies that were full of holes, internal contradictions, and unanticipated consequences.

Even when the policies were sound, Carter had little interest in mastering the details of execution. Apart from a few areas, mainly that of foreign policy, a president accomplishes very little simply by making the right decision; he must bring the public, Congress, or the permanent government over to his side if he wants to see his policies carried out. Carter took office with little background in this kind of persuasion, and his disinclination to squeeze his employees for every bit of knowledge they possessed about doing these jobs meant that one of his initiatives after another died soon after it was announced.

There was a good side to the kind of relationship Carter had with his staff: By keeping everyone in his own niche, not encouraging his economic adviser, for example, to criticize a proposal made by his foreign affairs adviser—as, say, FDR would not have hesitated to do—Carter created a White House with the least backbiting among staff members in modern memory.

The Bush administration was also remarkably free of internal strife, at least until its reelection effort faltered. Beyond a minor rivalry between Roger Porter and Richard Darman, occasional alliances of Scowcroft and Cheney against Baker, and general resentment of the arrogance of Sununu and Darman, harmony was the rule. Even the attacks on Sununu that resulted in his departure were largely orchestrated outside the White House by Robert Teeter, Ed Rollins, and unhappy Cabinet members.

Rivalry for the president's ear is the reason backbiting has been so common in other administrations. The Johnson White House saw many such rivalries; perhaps the most intense was between Marvin Watson and Bill Moyers. Under Nixon, Colson clashed with Haldeman and Ehrlichman; under Ford, Hartman with Cheney; and from the 1960 campaign until Kennedy's death, Richard Goodwin and Theodore Sorensen were rivals for the role of chief speech writer and chief brain, with Sorensen winning most of the time.

The most absurd rivalry arose during the Reagan administration, pitting Larry Speakes against David Gergen. It featured such shenanigans as Speakes's instructing his staff to adjust the height of the rostrum in the White House press room so as to make the very tall Gergen look even more giraffe-like.

Sometimes the result of such rivalry can be healthy for the president and the country—as it was much of the time under Roosevelt—but this is seldom the case when the rivals try to outdo one another not in force of argument, but in effort to please. At the court of King James I, the Catholic faction, finding the king between favorites and knowing his weakness for handsome young men, kept thrusting a lovely young male from the ranks across the king's path in the hope of gaining the most influence at court. Under Lyndon Johnson, the technique appears to have been rather more dull. The basic method, according to George Reedy, who was Johnson's press secretary and later wrote a fine book, *The Twilight of the Presidency*, was "to be present either personally or by a proxy piece of paper when good news arrives and to be certain someone else is present when the news is bad."

Albert Speer has written of a court that, while more grotesque, was yet similar to the White House in the behavior of its members: "The powerful men under Hitler were jealously watching each other. Bormann followed the simple principle of always remaining in the closest proximity to the source of all grace and favor. He accompanied Hitler to the Berghof and on trips, and in the Chancellery never left his side until Hitler went to bed in the early morning hours. . . ."

Jack Valenti took just this route to power in Johnson's administration. Such a relationship can deprive a person of his critical faculties, as Valenti exhibited when he announced he could sleep better at night knowing Johnson was president. And consider the account of National Security Council meetings during the same administration by Chester Cooper in his book *The Lost Crusade*:

"The president, in due course, would announce his decision and then poll everyone in the room—council members, their assistants, and members of the White House and NSC staff. 'Mr. Secretary, do you agree with the decision?' 'Yes, Mr. President.' 'Mr. X, do you agree?' 'I agree, Mr. President.' During the process, I would frequently fall into Walter Mitty–like fantasy: When my turn came, I would rise to my feet, slowly look around the room, and then directly at the president, and say very quietly and emphatically, 'Mr. President, gentlemen, I most definitely do *not* agree.' But I was removed from my trance when I heard the president's voice saying, 'Mr. Cooper, do you agree?' And out would come, 'Yes, Mr. President, I agree.'"

When John Sununu was asked if he spoke his mind to George Bush, he replied, "Not very often and only when asked." The government is not going to work very well if the president's principal aide hesitates to say what he thinks to his boss. Even when there is dissent, it will be quickly withdrawn—as was Colin Powell's argument against war in the Gulf—when the president indicates that he is coming to another conclusion.

I should acknowledge that an aide who knows his president well and who has a reasonable amount of courage can acquire techniques for telling the president he is wrong. For example, when John Kennedy would come up with a terrible idea, Ted Sorensen used to say, "That sounds like something Dick Nixon would have suggested."

If presidents have suffered from too much heel-clicking obeisance from their staffs, most felt they could use a lot more from the cabinet and bureaucracy. But the nature of organizational life dictates that the departments and their secretaries often will not want to give the president what he thinks he needs.

The president's interest is in performance: Four years after his election, he must again go to the voters and be able to show that his government has done the job. The departments' interest is not in performance but, of course, in their own survival. Only a handful of appointees at the very top are likely to care about the survival of the administration, or to imagine that, before his term is up, the president will have a clear enough view of what they've actually been doing to tell the difference between cooperation and obstruction. A secretary of labor may care more about the good opinion of the president of the AFL-CIO than he does about that of the president of the United States since simple political reality may dictate that the latter will have to keep a labor secretary who has the union's support. More common is the case of the department or agency head who, in order to win the loyalty of his subordinates, adopts their views as his own and champions their cause to the president.

Suppose the president determines that a drastic reorganization of the Department of Commerce to reduce the number of its programs is vital to the national interest. Naturally, this decision will be opposed by many individuals and groups: the secretary of commerce; the department's employees and their families; the congressmen whose committees oversee Commerce—and whose domains would shrink along with the department; and in all likelihood the lobbyists who deal with Commerce, who usually prefer to keep the government operating in its old, ineffective ways rather than risk any change.

Another reason the White House staff has to run the cabinet is that many of the nation's most serious problems cut across cabinet lines. Obviously, to wage a war against poverty one has to oversee programs run by Labor, Health and Human Services, Housing and Urban Development, and Agriculture. An antidrug program necessarily involves the Coast Guard and the Customs Bureau as well as the Drug Enforcement Agency.

As each administration becomes aware of these facts of life, there is a tendency to exert ever stronger control from the White House, with final policies being worked out there instead of at the cabinet level. This tendency leads to an amusing spectacle that is played out as a continuing drama when each new administration comes to town, as the president denounces the previous administration's centralization of power in the White House and says it will never happen again.

At a press conference the day after the 1976 election, Carter said: "I would choose secretaries of Agriculture, the Treasury, of Defense, HEW, HUD, and others who are completely competent to run their own departments. I would not try to run these departments from the White House. The White House staff would be serving in a staff capacity—not in an administrative capacity." Then the old cycle began again. By the middle of 1979, newspapers were full of stories about how the Carter administration was firing cabinet members and reasserting authority over the executive branch. In 1981 Reagan began his administration with the same ringing endorsement of cabinet government, and the cycle was on its way to being repeated once again. But by July 18, 1982, the *Washington Post* was saying, "Rather than the corporate-style cabinet government promised by Reagan during the 1980 presidential campaign, most important decisions are made among the small group of White House advisers."

The administration immediately preceding Carter's had staged the same. When Gerald Ford became president, he announced he would have no chief of staff. Instead, the lines of communication would radiate from him to his cabinet and senior staff like "the spokes of a wheel." Chaos was the result. Ford's time was frittered away in pointless meetings because no one was there to keep people from making appointments with the president merely to demonstrate their access to him.

Things changed, however. In 1975 Ford made Dick Cheney chief of staff. When Cheney left office he was presented with an object labeled THE SPOKES OF THE WHEEL—A RARE FORM OF ARTISTRY CONCEIVED BY DONALD RUMSFELD BUT MODIFIED BY DICK CHENEY. It was a bicycle wheel with all but one of the spokes twisted and disconnected. Cheney left it for his successor, Hamilton Jordan, along with a note warning him to beware of the spokes of the wheel.

The cabinet and the bureaucracy may be hard for the president to control, but they are as pliable as putty compared with Congress. With few exceptions, such as the beginning stages of implementing the New Deal (1933–36), the Great

Society (1964–66), and Reaganomics (1981), congressmen have devoted themselves to thwarting the will of whoever happens to be residing at 1600 Pennsylvania Avenue, often without regard to whether he is a member of their party or not.

Congressmen, like the president, need to be reelected; and again, like the president, to be reelected they must perform. But the kind of performance required of them is much different from what is demanded of the president: The president is asked to solve major national and world problems, whereas congressmen are asked to solve individual problems their constituents have with the government. The president must bring groups together in a broad coalition to support his programs; congressmen simply avoid offending their constituents so they won't vote against them.

It is this fear of offending that makes congressmen especially vulnerable to the persuasion of lobbyists, who can threaten to withhold their groups' votes or campaign contributions—or worse, give them to their opponents. Thus it is through congressmen that lobbyists usually influence the president. The president has much less reason to fear the ten-vote loss that haunts the dreams of congressmen from districts where the total vote may be less than 1 percent of that cast in a presidential race. He may be willing to resist one group's special pleadings in order to serve the national interest. That's why the White House ranks sixth on the lobbyist's target list. But if an interest group has gotten to, say, a committee chairman who controls the fate of legislation important to the president, the president listens.

But this also suggests the best way for a president to deal with Congress: by making himself the most effective lobbyist of all. There are two ways to do this, that of FDR and that of LBJ.

The FDR way was to mobilize the public through such devices as the famous fireside chats. Roosevelt spoke to the people; the people then spoke to Congress. In the period from 1933 to 1936, only a very brave congressman—or one from a safe Republican district—dared to oppose FDR, and an unprecedented amount of legislation was enacted at the president's urging. Fear of FDR's wrath (and, consequently, of losing the public's support and votes) kept Congress in line until Roosevelt first angered a large segment of the public by trying to pack the Supreme Court with his supporters and then attempted to purge the congressmen who had opposed him. The effort was a total flop, and FDR never again had such an easy time with Congress. Reagan's charm and speaking ability, which were comparable to FDR's, brought success for his programs during his first term. But his grip on the public began to slip as people began to realize that his grip on the issues was, unlike FDR's, slim indeed.

LBJ, by contrast, was incapable of mobilizing the masses. His formal speeches were dull beyond belief. He was, however, a master at one-on-one cajolery and tireless in its practice. Few congressmen could resist his combination of passionate persuasion, down-home humor, and not-so-subtle arm-twisting, which helped make the period from 1964 to 1966 probably the second most productive in legislative history. His success came to an end when he alienated much of the public with his policy of escalation in Vietnam, and many of his congressional supporters were defeated in the 1966 election.

Alexander Hamilton predicted in *The Federalist*, number 69, that the office of president "would amount to nothing more than the supreme command and direction of the military and naval forces." The domestic power of the president has grown since those days, but it is still far less than his power in the area of national security. An interesting illustration of just how weak a president can be on the domestic front comes from the later years of Johnson's presidency, after LBJ had lost his clout with Congress. In August 1967, Johnson decided that federally owned land in the cities should be used to solve the housing problem. His idea was to get cities to build "new towns" within their limits, using federal, state, and local money left over from existing programs so that Congress—which in its prevailing anti-Johnson mood probably would not have consented—wouldn't even have to be consulted.

But he still had to deal with local mayors and city councils, who proved to be just as recalcitrant as Congress. To top it off, the General Services Administration refused to give away the land without congressional authorization. So not only did he have to persuade local governments to build the homes, he also had to persuade them to buy the land. They refused to do either.

At the same time, as commander in chief of the armed forces, Johnson had five hundred thousand men carrying out extensive search-and-destroy operations in Vietnam. In that area he had power—he could push buttons and something happened. On the home front, pushing buttons produced nothing but a flurry of activity in his own staff.

Similarly, George Bush may have been tempted to use the military against Iraq because in so doing he could appear bold and decisive, whereas boldness and decisiveness were definitely not among the traits the public had seen him display in handling the savings and loan crisis or during the budget debacle of the summer of 1990. There is no question that the focus on the Gulf took his son Neil's participation in the S&L scandal off the front pages.

The fact that the button labeled DEFENSE or NATIONAL SECURITY produces results is therefore a mixed blessing. From the Ellsberg break-in to the Bay of Pigs incident to the Vietnam War to Iran-contra, excess after excess has been committed in the name of national security. Even in the case of Watergate, generally thought to be a purely domestic tragedy, the smoking gun of the cover-up was Nixon's misuse of his authority to protect national security—that is, his order to Haldeman to have the CIA tell the FBI to stop investigating because national security was involved.

Pressure to cover up bad news, to avoid "leaks" of truths unpleasant to the president, has been a constant source of evil in the culture of the White House. Even in the Bay of Pigs episode, for which Kennedy bravely accepted complete responsibility after the event, the cover-up mentality had a lot to do with how the failure happened in the first place. A careful reading of the histories of the incident strongly suggests that Kennedy actually thought the invasion was a bad idea. But he also thought that canceling it would show weakness. So rather than facing the issue squarely, he waffled and postponed. And rather than debating the pluses and minuses of the invasion with people who were likely to see and point out the latter, he let himself be bamboozled by CIA director Allen Dulles and his deputy, Richard Bissell, who saw only the pluses. They also played on Kennedy's fear that a cancellation could not be covered up.

There were two important meetings about the planned invasion in the spring of 1961. In the first, the planners of the operation dominated, and Dulles skillfully exacerbated Kennedy's fear of exposure by warning him that if he called off the operation it would mean that trained guerrillas would be "wandering around the country telling the country what they have been doing." In the second meeting Kennedy assembled a more reliable crew, but he made sure he wouldn't get any useful advice from them by going around the room and demanding from everyone present a simple go or no-go opinion. The two men high in the administration who were not obsessed with the fear of appearing soft, Adlai Stevenson and Chester Bowles, pointedly had no role in the deliberations. Stevenson was kept in the dark throughout, and Bowles's memorandum opposing the invasion never got past Dean Rusk's desk.

When Kennedy finally made the crucial decisions about the invasion, he did so in solitude and gave his orders over the phone. Alone in his office, he called Bissell and told him to cut back the planned level of air support for the operation; alone again, he called Bissell and told him to start the invasion; and alone at his country house, he called an aide and canceled a second air strike at the landing site, thereby completely assuring the operation's failure.

The only good that came out of the fiasco was that Kennedy learned some lessons that helped him deal more successfully with the biggest crisis of his administration. By the time he discovered in October 1962 that the Russians were secretly installing missiles in Cuba, he had communicated to the national security bureaucracy that he did not reward those who lied to him. Dulles was out; so was Bissell. And this time Kennedy cross-examined each of his advisers to bring out any hidden assumptions or subtle doubts. He also broadened the group to include a dozen advisers like his brother who were outside the chain of command.

Robert Kennedy was given the most sensitive task of the missile crisis negotiations, letting Soviet ambassador Anatoly Dobrynin know that we were going to pull our missiles out of Turkey. This gave Khrushchev the *quid* he needed for all the *quo* he was having to swallow. But John Kennedy was so anxious to appear tough that he never let the American people know about the assurance to Dobrynin—indeed, he denounced Adlai Stevenson for suggesting such a course.

Another serious problem the White House faces is the lack of institutional memory. Whereas a few survivors from the Reagan administration stayed on when Bush became president because Bush had been vice president under Reagan, there were of course no holdovers from Carter to Reagan. Reagan even fired his predecessor's clerical staff, while Carter removed the White House files for his presidential library. The law has since been changed so that duplicate files must remain for the new administration, but there can still be a complete purge of personnel. For this reason, although I usually favor less civil service in government, I strongly believe the White House staff should be approximately one-third civil servants to provide continuity from one administration to another.

The life span of an administration is also shorter than you may think. Assuming that Bill Clinton is reelected in 1996, he should realize that he will have only two even possibly effective years left in his presidency. Because the Twenty-second Amendment to the Constitution prevents a president from running for a third term, presidential power declines dramatically in the final two years of his second term. The prospect of his favor thus comes to mean less and less to those who want government jobs and contracts, while the press, which values its White House sources too much to criticize them in the early years of an administration, will now aggressively pursue any hint of scandal as the value of its sources declines. Good appointees are also hard to find because people don't want to join an administration that's on its last legs.

Recent history presents each president with an agenda. There are problems on his desk when he arrives, like the Middle East crisis that has been waiting for each of the last four presidents. Daily events produce new problems that must be faced, and ceremonial functions, from laying a wreath to greeting a prime minister, take place in which the president feels obliged to participate. And every day there are the memoranda, the telephone calls, and the meetings that tell him what the rest of the government thinks his agenda should be.

We need a president who refuses to be ruled by the agendas of others. We need a president who has a program of his own, who looks beyond the problems that are obvious today to those that could confound us tomorrow. But having a program is itself not enough. We have to take a hard look at how sound the program is, at how much sense it makes. After all, Ronald Reagan had a program, but it happened to be the wrong one. The result was severe economic distress for the lower middle class and the poor.

In addition to looking at the program a presidential candidate offers, we should look at the character of the man behind it. Character is the ability to rise above the forces that keep us from thinking clearly—not only about what will work, but about what is right. Johnson and Nixon displayed a crucial lack of it in yielding to the need to appear tough, which kept them from steering the right course in Southeast Asia.

Kennedy turned the Bay of Pigs failure into the success of the missile crisis the following year by overcoming his fear of seeming to be soft in time to tell the Russians he would remove our missiles from Turkey. If only he had not been afraid of letting the public know what he had done! The tragic result of this fear was that people saw the missile crisis as a triumph of toughness and saw the lesson as a need to demonstrate our "resolve" in Vietnam. One wonders how many lives could have been saved if Kennedy had told the truth about his dovish gesture. Maybe then he could have told the public what in fact he told only two men: that he thought Vietnam was a mistake and planned to pull out after the 1964 election.

Robert Kennedy finally revealed his visit to Dobrynin in a book published shortly after his assassination in 1968, although Ted Sorensen, John Kennedy's former aide who edited the manuscript, managed to obscure the facts so that they were still not widely known until 1987. But even Bob Kennedy's muted revelations came more than five years after the event—and three years and thousands of deaths after we had demonstrated our resolve in Vietnam by the escalation of 1965. It is hard to learn from history if your leaders hide it from you.

A WAY OUT

The title of this book may be misleading. The truth is that Washington doesn't really work. The government is solving far too few of the nation's problems. The question, of course, is what—if anything—can be done. My answer is simple: Let's try democracy. Too many of the decisions that govern our lives are made by bureaucrats and lobbyists who are not accountable to the people, or by elected officials who have not won on level playing fields.

As practically everyone who has thought about the matter at all realizes, true democracy depends on fair elections, which means we must eliminate the power of money over politics. But what practically no one seems to understand is that democracy also requires a government that is accountable. Today's bureaucrats aren't accountable to the people because they can't be fired by the elected representatives of the people. If elections are going to mean anything—and they often mean nothing because they do not change the permanent government—the administration must be given the authority to hire and fire not just cabinet members and agency heads, but also enough other officials, high and low, to allow the president to move the machinery of government. To provide greater grass-roots involvement in the federal bureaucracy, power over a reasonable number of federal appointments within congressional districts

159

should be shared with the local congressmen, or local party officials if the congressman is not in the president's party, just as administrations have traditionally shared with senators the power to appoint federal judges and U.S. attorneys within a senator's state—or as your congressman chose the local postmaster back in the days when your mail was delivered twice a day. Just as back then, if your postman spends his time reading his mail instead of delivering yours, you will know where the blame belongs.

If we are going to truly reform the American system of government, we need more politics rather than less—more good people running for office and helping other good people run for office. If you never again want to choose between a Michael Dukakis and a George Bush, you must make sure you have a greater choice from among those involved in politics. This in turn means offering decent rewards for such involvement. Today a person who starts out in politics has only a tiny field of opportunity for service in the national government—president, senator, representative, and just two thousand federal appointive positions. He or she could get a job in state or local government, but such jobs are also mostly dominated by the civil service, leaving few openings to reward political work. Of course, the campaign worker could be paid a salary. Unfortunately, that kind of compensation increases campaign costs while failing to attract persons with the substantive interest in government we want participants in politics to have. But what if we opened up hundreds of thousands of federal jobs to political appointees, replacing roughly 50 percent of all the federal government's civilian employees as jobs come open through normal attrition? Give the new people two-and-a-half-year appointments, with a limit of ten years on the time they would be permitted to remain in government. This plan would:

• bring people with real-world experience into government
• attract a different kind of person, the risk-taker, who is not interested in job security and would therefore be less cautious and self-protective than a civil servant

• provide a legitimate reward for political participation and thus attract more people to political activity. (The reward would be legitimate because the unqualified would not profit from it. Your sister Susie, who can't type more than twenty words a minute, wouldn't get that government typing job no matter how hard she worked on your campaign)

• give presidents the patronage needed to rebuild the political parties as bulwarks against the threat of interest group politics

• send back to the nation as members of the voting public literally millions of people who have personal knowledge of how the government doesn't work, of the reforms that are needed to make it function, and of how to bring them about

But suppose the present administration is permitted to begin making such appointments now, and you're a member of the opposing party and think that's terrible. Some bad choices might be made; that I can't dispute. But you could vote in your candidate in the next election and replace all the bad appointees—remember, every one of them would come up for reappointment within two and a half years—with people dedicated to the program of the new president. Because we could see the difference this new blood would make, more of us would be concerned about voting and about voting wisely. Keep in mind that the last president who did great things was FDR, who hired not the two thousand employees recent presidents have had power to choose, but two and a half million. We don't have to go that far, but it does suggest the direction in which we need to travel.

All this is not to say that I think the career civil servant serves no useful purpose. If I felt that way, I wouldn't advocate retaining half of them, as I do. They provide continuity, institutional memory, and insurance against the excesses of politicians. All of these are valuable functions. But we also need people with other virtues in our government, the kind of people short-term appointments would attract. Most of all we need to offer the incentives that will attract people who can revitalize our political system. If we don't want a system that runs on money, then we have to offer something else. What is better to offer to those who push doorbells and hand out leaflets than the opportunity to participate in putting into effect the programs they have campaigned for?

If we had millions of such persons who had served in government and then returned to their homes as citizens and voters, we would have a nation far better equipped to make budget cuts when they are needed. We would have a public whose members wouldn't have to guess where the fat is because they would know exactly where to find it. Similarly, they would have a sense of what programs are working well and deserve more money. We would have an electorate that knows the score.

Finally, we would have people in government who, because they've spent most of their lives on the outside, would have genuine empathy for the problems of those on the outside. The lack of such empathy has been the most glaring deficiency of the bureaucracy since I have been in Washington. And I fear it will only become worse because the mindless Reaganite attack on the bureaucracy has exacerbated the civil servant's tendency toward self-protection, just as did the equally mindless McCarthyite attack of the fifties.

In *Elrod* v. *Burns* and again in *Branti* v. *Finkel*, the Supreme Court held that public officials below the policymaking level can't be fired on political grounds because that would penalize them for their ideas. The court maintained that this rule applies even when the officials were hired as political appointees. Obviously, the right to free speech should not include the right to a permanent government job. The point of democracy is to let voters remove officials whose ideas they don't like. If we are to have a government that really works, it is important that voters have the power to remove those who execute policies as well as those who make them. The only exceptions should be the employees we choose to protect from dismissal by making them tenured civil servants. Justice Antonin Scalia wrote a brilliant dis-

sent to *Rutan* v. *Republican Party of Illinois*, a 1991 case on
political patronage and the spoils system, that showed he
understood these points. While in general he is much too
conservative for my taste, I pray that on this issue his
reasoning will ultimately prevail.

With a genuinely accountable government, congressmen
and their staffs will no longer have to devote 80 percent of
their time to the kind of trivial constituent service that is
required to correct the errors of an inefficient and indiffer-
ent bureaucracy. Instead they will be able to concentrate on
their proper duties, which include determining what new
laws are needed and what old laws should be changed as
well as overseeing the activities of the executive branch.
Because members of Congress and the president would
share the appointing authority for some federal officials
working at the grass-roots level, they should finally be able
to bridge much of the communication gap between the people at the bottom and those at the top, which results in
those at the top seldom knowing the truth about what goes
on down below and therefore not knowing what laws to pass
or what orders to give.

It is equally important that this information reach those
on the outside, that the people find out what's going on at
both the top and the bottom—whether it's what John Kennedy did about the Turkish missiles or whether the fact that
that social security check is missing is an isolated mistake
or part of a larger problem that government should do something about.

The main responsibility for providing this information
belongs to the press. To fulfill its role, the press needs to
develop a new breed of reporters who have either worked
in government and know its problems firsthand or who have
studied the history of the American political system and
the lessons of its successes and failures—who have the de-
scriptive skill to report accurately on what the government
is doing, the analytical skill to figure out how what it is
doing can be done better (or whether it should be done at

all), and the literary skill to make the description and analysis something that people will read and remember. I don't think that every reporter must be a Tolstoy or a Dickens. I do think that reporters and their employers must raise and broaden their aspirations so that success on our great papers comes to mean not only rooting out a scandal or getting a politician indicted, but telling us how it can be made right.

None of this will make any difference, however, until a majority of us, reporters included, are willing to renounce our own roles in the game of make-believe. This will be hard for the reporter who wants to believe that covering presidential press conferences is important. It will be hard for nearly everyone, in fact, because most of us have a stake in make-believe. The congressmen who only pretend to consider serious reduction of government spending reflect our own reluctance to jeopardize the loophole or expenditure that benefits us. The main reason the lobbies usually win is that each of them represents at least some of us.

The only time we seem passionate about making government work is when its help is needed by our own interest group. The result is a nation dominated by single-issue partisanship, a partisanship that is fueled by the adversarialism of our lawyer-saturated culture and that encourages selfishness and blind indifference to arguments and facts inconsistent with the specific axes we happen to be grinding. What is wrong with Washington, then, is what is wrong with the rest of us. It won't be cured until we have a rebirth of patriotism—or if that word embarrasses you, a willingness to put the welfare of the national community above our own.

BIBLIOGRAPHY

The books consulted for this edition and listed below were for the most part published after the first edition of *How Washington Really Works* appeared in 1980. Where a book is not well known or its title not self-explanatory, I have added a brief explanation of its contents.

CHAPTER 1: THE PRESS

Auletta, Ken. *Three Blind Mice: How the TV Networks Lost Their Way.* New York: Random House, 1991. Examines news coverage by the major television networks.

Bagdikian, Ben H. *The Media Monopoly.* 3rd ed. Boston: Beacon, 1990.

Blumenthal, Sidney. *The Permanent Campaign.* New York: Simon & Schuster, 1982.

Braestrup, Peter. *Big Story.* 2 vols. Boulder, Colo.: Westview, 1977.

Crouse, Timothy. *The Boys on the Bus: Riding with the Campaign Press Corps.* New York: Random House, 1972.

Halberstam, David. *The Powers That Be.* New York: Knopf, 1979.

Hertsgaard, Mark. *On Bended Knee: The Press and the Reagan Presidency.* New York: Farrar, Straus & Giroux, 1988. How the press kowtows to the president.

Hess, Stephen. *Live! from Capitol Hill: Essays on Congress and the Media.* Washington, D.C.: Brookings Institution, 1991.

Sabato, Larry J. *Feeding Frenzy: How Attack Journalism Has Transformed American Politics.* New York: Free Press, 1991.

Schram, Martin. *The Great American Video Game.* New York: Morrow, 1987.

Speakes, Larry, and Robert Pack. *Speaking Out: The Reagan Presidency from Inside the White House.* New York: Scribner's, 1988.

Wakeman, Carolyn, ed. *The Media and the Gulf: A Closer Look.* Berkeley: University of California Graduate School of Journalism, 1991.

Weinberg, Steve. *Trade Secrets of Washington Journalists: How to Get the Facts About What's Going On in Washington.* Reston, Va.: Acropolis, 1981.

CHAPTER 2: LOBBIES

Hansen, John M. *Gaining Access: Congress and the Farm Lobby, 1919–1981.* Chicago: University of Chicago Press, 1991.

Hrebenar, Ronald J., and Ruth K. Scott. *Interest Group Politics in America.* Englewood Cliffs, N.J.: Prentice-Hall, 1982.

Kotz, Nick. *Wild Blue Yonder: Money, Politics, and the B-1 Bomber.* New York: Pantheon, 1988. A case study of how lobbyists influence decisions about national defense.

Wittenberg, Ernest, and Elizabeth Wittenberg. *How to Win in Washington: Very Practical Advice about Lobbying, the Grassroots, and the Media.* Cambridge, MA.: Basil Blackwell, 1989. Explains how Congress really works and what moves it to action.

Zorack, John L. *The Lobbying Handbook.* Washington, D.C.: Beacham, 1990.

CHAPTER 3: THE BUREAUCRACY

Glazer, Myron Peretz, and Penina Migdal Glazer. *The Whistleblowers: Exposing Corruption in Government and Industry.* New York: Basic Books, 1989.

Goodsell, Charles T. *The Case for Bureaucracy: A Public Administration Polemic.* 2nd ed. Chatham, N.J.: Chatham House, 1985.

Hirschman, Albert O. *Exit, Voice, and Loyalty: Responses to Decline in Firms, Organizations, and States.* Cambridge: Harvard University Press, 1969.

Johnson, Gail. *Recruiting, Retaining, and Motivating the Federal Workforce.* Westport, Conn.: Quorum, 1991.

Kaufman, Herbert, and Michael Couzens. *Administrative Feedback: Monitoring Subordinates' Behavior.* Washington, D.C.: Brookings Institution, 1973.

Lynn, Jonathan, and Antony Jay. *The Complete Yes Minister: The Diaries of a Cabinet Minister by the Right Hon. James Hacker, M.P.* London, England: British Broadcasting Corporation, 1982. The relationship between senior civil servants and elected officials.

Peters, Charles, and Taylor Branch, eds. *Blowing the Whistle: Dissent in the Public Interest.* New York: Praeger, 1972. A collection of articles from *The Washington Monthly.*

Peters, Charles, and Michael Nelson, eds. *The Culture of Bureaucracy.* New York: Holt, Rinehart & Winston, 1979. A collection of articles from *The Washington Monthly.*

Wilson, James Q. *Bureaucracy: What Government Agencies Do and Why They Do It.* New York: Basic Books, 1989.

CHAPTER 4: THE FOREIGN SERVICES

Bamford, James. *The Puzzle Palace: A Report on America's Most Secret Agency.* Boston: Houghton Mifflin, 1982. Inside the National Security Agency.

Herz, Martin F. *215 Days in the Life of an American Ambassador.* Washington, D.C.: Georgetown University School of Foreign Service, 1981.

Isaacson, Walter, and Evan Thomas. *The Wise Men: Six Friends and the World They Made.* New York: Simon & Schuster, 1986.

Kocher, Eric. *Foreign Intrigue: The Making and Unmaking of a Foreign Service Officer.* Far Hills, N.J.: New Horizon, 1990.

O'Toole, G. J. A. *Honorable Treachery: A History of U.S. Intelligence, Espionage, and Covert Action from the American Revolution to the CIA.* New York: Atlantic Monthly Press, 1991.

Paddock, William, and Elizabeth Paddock. *We Don't Know How: An Independent Audit of What They Call Success in Foreign Assistance.* Ames: Iowa State University Press, 1973. Bureaucratic problems in foreign aid, such as lack of institutional memory.

Rusk, Dean, and Richard Rusk. *As I Saw It.* Ed. Daniel S. Papp. New York: Norton, 1990.

Sheehan, Neil. *A Bright Shining Lie: John Paul Vann and America in Vietnam.* New York: Random House, 1988.

Snepp, Frank. *Decent Interval: An Insider's Account of Saigon's Indecent End.* New York: Random House, 1977.

Turner, Stansfield. *Terrorism and Democracy.* Boston: Houghton Mifflin, 1991.

CHAPTER 5: THE MILITARY

Fallows, James. *National Defense.* New York: Random House, 1981.

Gabriel, Richard A. and Paul L. Savage. *Crisis in Command: Mismanagement in the Army.* New York: Hill and Wang, 1979.

Kotz, Nick. *Wild Blue Yonder: Money, Politics, and the B-1 Bomber.* New York: Pantheon, 1988. See citation for ch. 2.

Luttwak, Edward. *The Pentagon and the Art of War: The Question of Military Reform.* New York: Simon & Schuster, 1984.

Woodward, Bob. *The Commanders.* New York: Simon & Schuster, 1991.

CHAPTER 6: COURTS AND REGULATORS

Brill, Steven, and Karen McCoy, eds. *Trial by Jury: The American Way of Justice Today.* New York: Touchstone, 1989.

Downie, Leonard, Jr. *Justice Denied: The Case for Reform of the Courts.* New York: Praeger, 1971.

Forer, Lois G. *The Death of the Law.* New York: McKay, 1975.

———. *Money and Justice: Who Owns the Courts?* New York: Norton, 1984.

———. *Unequal Protection: Women, Children, and the Elderly in Court.* New York: Norton, 1991.

Harris, Richard A., and Sidney M. Milkis. *The Politics of Regulatory Change: A Tale of Two Agencies.* New York: Oxford University Press, 1989.

Neely, Richard. *Why Courts Don't Work.* New York: McGraw-Hill, 1983.

Simon, James. *The Antagonists: Hugo Black, Felix Frankfurter and Civil Liberties in America.* New York: Simon & Schuster, 1989.

Strick, Anne. *Injustice for All: How Our Adversary System of Law*

Victimizes Us and Subverts True Justice. New York: Putnam's, 1977.

Sunstein, Cass R. *After the Rights Revolution: Reconceiving the Regulatory State.* Cambridge: Harvard University Press, 1990.

Woodward, Bob, and Scott Armstrong. *The Brethren.* New York: Simon & Schuster, 1979.

CHAPTER 7: CONGRESS

Drew, Elizabeth. *Senator.* New York: Simon & Schuster, 1978.

Elliott, Carl, Sr., and Mike D'Orso. *The Cost of Courage: The Journey of an American Congressman.* New York: Doubleday, 1992.

Fowler, Linda L., and Robert D. McClure. *Political Ambition: Who Decides to Run for Congress.* New Haven and London: Yale University Press, 1989.

Mayhew, David R. *Congress: The Electoral Connection.* New Haven: Yale University Press, 1974.

O'Neill, Tip, with William Novak. *Man of the House: The Life and Political Memoirs of Speaker Tip O'Neill.* New York: Random House, 1987.

Pitch, Anthony S. *Congressional Chronicles: Amusing and Amazing Anecdotes of the U.S. Congress and Its Members.* Potomac, Md.: Mino, 1990.

Sinclair, Barbara. *The Transformation of the U.S. Senate.* Baltimore: Johns Hopkins University Press, 1991.

Smith, Steven S. *Call to Order: Floor Politics in the House and Senate.* Washington, D.C.: Brookings Institution, 1989.

CHAPTER 8: THE WHITE HOUSE

Beschloss, Michael R. *The Crisis Years: Kennedy and Khrushchev, 1960–1963.* HarperCollins, 1991. An especially thorough account of the Cuban missile crisis is a highlight of this history of the relationship between Kennedy and Khrushchev.

Gulley, Bill, with Mary Ann Reese. *Breaking Cover.* New York: Simon & Schuster, 1980. The bureaucratic absurdities of life at the White House, recorded by the man who was in charge of distributing perks under four presidents.

Jordan, Hamilton. *Crisis: The Last Year of the Carter Presidency.* New York: Putnam's, 1982.

Neustadt, Richard E. *Presidential Power and the Modern Presidents: The Politics of Leadership from Roosevelt to Reagan.* New York: Free Press, 1990.

Patterson, Bradley H., Jr. *The Ring of Power: The White House Staff and Its Expanding Role in Government.* New York: Basic Books, 1988.

Schlesinger, Arthur M., Jr. *The Imperial Presidency.* Boston: Houghton Mifflin, 1973.

Shogan, Robert. *None of the Above: Why Presidents Fail—and What Can Be Done About It.* New York: New American Library, 1982.

Wyden, Peter. *Bay of Pigs: The Untold Story.* New York: Simon & Schuster, 1979.

RELATED READING

Peters, Charles, and Jonathan Alter. *Inside the System.* 5th ed. Englewood Cliffs, N.J.: Prentice-Hall, 1985. A collection of articles from *The Washington Monthly.*

Peters, Charles, and James Fallows. *The System.* New York: Praeger, 1976. Contains chapters on the presidency and the bureaucracy by Morton Halperin, on Congress by Jerome Waldie and Michael Green, on the courts by John MacKenzie, on the press by Fallows, and on lobbies by Peters.

Smith, Hedrick. *The Power Game: How Washington Works.* New York: Random House, 1989.

INDEX